The Business of Aspiration

How Social, Cultural, and Environmental Capital Changes Brands

ANA ANDJELIC

Routledge
Taylor & Francis Group

LONDON AND NEW YORK

First published 2021
by Routledge
2 Park Square, Milton Park, Abingdon, Oxon OX14 4RN

and by Routledge
52 Vanderbilt Avenue, New York, NY 10017

Routledge is an imprint of the Taylor & Francis Group, an informa business

British Library Cataloguing-in-Publication Data
A catalogue record for this book is available from the British Library

Library of Congress Cataloging-in-Publication Data
A catalog record has been requested for this book

ISBN: 978-0-367-55221-3 (hbk)
ISBN: 978-0-367-55440-8 (pbk)
ISBN: 978-1-003-09357-2 (ebk)

Typeset in Dante and Avenir
by codeMantra

To my grandmothers,

who didn't follow the rules

Contents

Preface

This book was finished in early April of 2020 in New York City, at the height of the global pandemic and in the epicenter of the US virus contagion.

Overnight, the city shut down, and with it all the benefits of having an easy access to culture, fine dining, art, theater, fitness, and nightlife evaporated. Our Dumbo apartment became very small once we had to spend majority of our time in it.

Five weeks into self-quarantine, I read *Financial Times'* Editor's Letter "How to Spend It". It asked, defensively, "What does a luxury magazine have to contribute to the world during a pandemic? To put it bluntly – who cares about expensive chairs?"

Turns out, a lot of people do. Luxury domesticity, a term coined by author and consultant Venkatesh Rao during our email exchange, is gaining steam as a trend. Rao and I were going back and forth about what's aspirational at the moment, and what kind of aspiration we can expect once the pandemic is over. We finally agreed on the return of traditional luxury, and its stability, permanence, and security. Kanye West tapped into it when he bought a ranch in Wyoming. He's building a "Yeezy campus" and a "paradigm shift for humanity" there. Given that Kanye has a track record of paradigm shifts in music, fashion, and culture, I eagerly await its completion.

Luxury domesticity describes the tangible assets that we all wish we had right now: spacious real estate, a coronavirus test, private planes, yachts, rare whiskeys. It also refers to the status-signaling behaviors like cooking, decorating, exercising. We can buy truffles directly from Michelin-starred restaurant suppliers, and we can take a free live-stream cooking lessons from Michelin-starred chefs. The promise of fine dining experience at our own home, paired with the meditative pleasure of making food with our own hands, may keep us inside forever.

"Why do we live in a small apartment in London? Why do we live in England? Can we live somewhere nicer?" asked my friend Rachel Arthur, a sustainability and innovation consultant. She currently works remotely, and has captured the mood of a lot of urbanites, who increasingly consider the dreaded suburbs, slower pace of life, and practicing domesticity.

Remote work may speed up spreading out of the urban population. But offices are not only about work, and work is not the sole thing that keeps us in the cities: there's going out, culture, dining, fashion, and just the sheer pleasure of neighborhoods and communities. They will emerge from this crisis different than before. I used to go out a lot to Lucky Strike, a self-described "shabby-chic neighborhood bistro" on Grand Street. It's closing. Smaller, independent fashion labels, galleries, and tradesmen make the cultural fabric of cities like New York or London diverse, creative, and exciting. A lot of them won't be there anymore when we finally reemerge.

The same goes for brands. Crises are great truth-tellers, and how brands behave right now will either be a wind in their sails or it's going to haunt them for a really long time. There's plenty of confusion about the appropriate brand behavior at the moment. Big brands uniformly churn out public service announcement-like creative campaigns that heavily lean on somber piano music, photos of empty streets, and Zoom family gatherings. Smaller brands are more creative: they activate their communities, live-stream home exercise and cooking lessons, partner up with other small brands to lighten up their customers' lives, and shower their customers with compassion, recipes, and tunes of chanting monks. Not every brand reads the room: some are still pitching Mother's Day sales and suggest spending government stimulus money on clothes shopping.

Brands discovered that they need a more coordinated and less siloed approach. At the time of severe marketing budget cuts, the way to maintain a relationship with customers is through inter-departmental collaboration and reliance on each other's strengths. This is a more resilient and robust brand model, where marketing works in sync with operations, logistics, finance, customer service, and internal and external communications.

The future of brand strategy is shaping up in front of our eyes. Cultural, social, and environmental capital rises and falls in value daily. As our values rearrange themselves, so does the business of aspiration.

Ana Andjelic
New York City, April 2020

Introduction
The modern aspiration economy

A disheveled young man, in a dirty T-shirt and with a face covered with tar, is molding a blade in a fire pit. His south-east London workshop is nested under a railway arch. It's filled with smoke. Walls are dark with grime.

This isn't a scene from London circa the Industrial Revolution. It is a scene circa now, and the young man is James Ross-Harris, one of the three founders and bladesmiths of Blenheim Forge knives. Influenced by the simplicity and rusticity of wabi-sabi, Blenheim Forge places traditional Japanese methods at the heart of how they manufacture their knives: adapted from a traditional Japanese sword-making design, they fuse three layers of high carbon, Hitachi blue paper and Damascus steel. Each knife is handmade to order.

More than a century ago, American economist and sociologist Thorstein Veblen linked desirability of a good to its price: as the price increases, so does the desirability and demand. A fitness class or a luxury handbag is more desirable if expensive; if their price drops, so does consumer demand for them. Veblen goods defy the traditional economic logic where a price of a good or service is inversely correlated with its demand. Instead, they are socially positional: high-end fashion, watches, cars, wine, organic food, travel experiences, and practices of self-actualization visibly and publicly convey the appearance of success, wealth, status, identity, and personal enlightenment.

Blenheim Forge knives are a post-Veblen good. Coveting a Blenheim Forge knife has nothing to do with its price, and status of those who buy them is not linked to wealth.

Welcome to the modern aspiration economy

Modern aspiration economy is anchored not in accumulation and display of possessions or even experiences, but of social capital, environmental credits, and cultural savviness (Currid-Halkett, 2017; Eckhardt, 2020). The fuel of social, cultural, and environmental capital is art, design, architecture, fashion, food, music, travel, self-transformation, wellness, sustainable living. This modern capital is also rooted in FOMO (fear of missing out) and in being in the know: in knowing about obscure locations offering transformative travel experiences, in the ability to decode subtle brand signals or learn about coveted vintage and streetwear drops, and to own limited-edition objects that come with a story and represent a domain of culture (e.g. streetwear, vintage, minimalism, membership in a community) or nature (e.g. handmade, farming, horticulture). There's status in membership in a community, or in the ability to attract and command attention on social media by accumulating likes and followers (Eckhardt, 2019).

This new social, cultural, and environmental capital changes the way businesses and entire markets operate, and here you will learn how your brand can trade in this new capital.

Not long ago, wearing real fur was a signal of wealth and status. Now, it's a signal of ignorance. In contrast, fake fur is inexpensive, but it displays status lent by awareness about climate crisis and importance of sustainability.

Once reliable signals of class and status, traditional luxury brands can now be rented and resold. Anyone can walk around in a Gucci outfit. This upends the notion of a Veblen good. A Veblen good is something whose desirability increases with price. But an artisanal knife can today be deemed more desirable than a Louis Vuitton bag, and eating in zero-waste restaurants signals status more than staying in a Four Seasons hotel. Class is decoupled from money: inexpensive goods and activities – like wearing clothes made of recycled materials, meditation, or having plant-based diet, are modern status symbols. When consumers buy non-Genetically Modified and ask questions about where something was made and by whom, they create a modern class distinction through their wokeness.

"Stay at home," urged Instagram influencers during the deadly coronavirus pandemic. Ethical stance, restraint, displays of kindness and generosity, and positive social values replaced wealth as signals of status. In the modern aspiration economy, Greta Thunberg, a teenager whose cause and moral conviction puts the rest of us to shame, enjoys elite status. Modern aspirants are environmentalists, influencers, fans, sneakerheads, hobbyists, and collectors. They covet a vintage Chanel jacket because they know it had been worn by Vanessa Paradis in the film "Heartbreaker." Knowledge gives products value, and creates a divide between those in the know and those who neither have this Chanel jacket nor know that Vanessa Paradis wore it.

Modern aspiration economy splits the traditional territory of aspiration in two. Perhaps the most astute way of capturing the past decade's bifurcation of aspiration is a neon sign saying "You are obviously in the wrong place" featured at Off-White's 2016 Fall-Winter runway show. Referencing a line from the movie "Pretty Woman," the sign captures the fact that there was hardly a period where aspiration meant more, and less. The use of the term expanded to include brands from Rolex to Louis Vuitton to Cartier to Nike to Sonos to Shinola to Supreme to Kim Jones' Dior collaborations. It also constricted to ephemerals like time, space, privacy, self-actualization, belonging, human originality, and artisanship. The Louvre Abu Dhabi's "10,000 Years of Luxury" exhibition ends with an hourglass.

On the one hand, there is Big Luxury. Like Big Pharma or Big Media, Big Luxury is commercial, and its goal is to push consumers to buy more. This is the domain of streetwear collaborations and "premium mediocre" (Rao, 2017), which emphasizes merch and logos that turn everyone willing to spend $600 on a T-shirt, a branded hat, or a belt into a luxury consumer. In the Big Luxury, a high-end piece of jewelry is selected to go with the latest sneakers or a handbag. A taped banana is art. A hoodie is the status symbol. As sociologist Georg Simmel observed a long time ago, fashion raises "even the unimportant individual by making them the representative of a class, the embodiment of a joint spirit." So does Dior x Stüssy.

In contrast to Big Luxury are the likes of Blenheim Forge, who identify with the exceptional artisanal work. "We are not luxury," claims the revered leather goods house Hermès. "We are high quality." Modern aspiration champions' displays of human originality. This isn't a world of goods and commodities, but the world of handcrafted objects. Detailing how things are made – sustainably, transparently, and according to a specific artisanal tradition – is a distinction that producers use to attract modern aspirants. Just look at *Financial Times'* How to Spend It, also known as "the shopping list for the 1 percent." It is full of features on makers, hikes in Nicaragua, Yule logs, and admiration for limited-edition, low-tech displays of human creativity.

The modern aspiration economy transforms the role and meaning of brands. What consumers value and how they distinguish themselves from others and convey their status are now different than it was a 100, or even ten years ago. When the consumer value calculus is different, so is the business. Desirability of something is today decoupled from its price, and its access is decoupled from wealth. Instead, it's coupled with social capital, environmental creds, cultural savviness, a story, belonging, and its transformative potential to make us better humans. What consumers value and how, what they pay money and attention to, and how they distinguish themselves from others and convey their status are different than they were at the time of Veblen. It's different than even ten years ago.

This book explores how the modern aspiration economy changes brand strategy. In here, you can expect to find analysis, examples, and tools of how to use the modern aspiration economy to shift your brand narrative and competitive strategy, create and distribute brand symbols, and ensure that your products and services create both monetary and moral value.

It is not only business-savvy, but also socially urgent that brands start trading in the modern aspiration economy. Overproduction and air travel are killing our planet, and social media addiction and busyness are killing us.

Accumulating commodities and counting air miles and social media likes are aspiration symbols that reward the bad behavior of companies and individuals. We need a new narrative of success, and brands are uniquely positioned to carry it out. By their very nature, brands trade in status: they promise us to be younger, more attractive, smarter, happier, more accomplished, richer. For the longest time, brands operated according to Veblen logic that status is linked to wealth and desirability to price. Now we all have the opportunity to flip the script and link worth and values to our business success.

In this book, you will learn how to create, distribute, and deliver social, cultural, and environmental capital when making your business and brand decisions:

- Pay attention to how consumers spend their time and money, how they relate to each other, and how these social processes create the new forms of cultural, social, and environmental capital.
- Understand that values create value and that ethics creates efficiency: replace traditional status symbols and narratives of success and put forward environmentalism, social responsibility, and cultural knowledge as the new one.
- Detect the social, cultural, and economic mood by spotting on inversions, contradictions, coincidences, and oddities in consumer behavior and culture.
- Address collective versus individual dimensions of consumer behavior: shift from targeting individuals to targeting communities.
- Build taste collectives around commercial symbols and grow through niches.
- Understand the benefits and differences between the three models of social influence and turn your products into shareable social symbols.
- Capitalize on social mimicry in the way you come up and scale your creative output.

- Root your brand strategy in one or more of the four Cs: community, content, curation, and collaborations.
- Understand that people consume through collecting: sneakers, likes, references, memes, points for minimalistic living.
- Learn what business strategy can borrow from sociology.

In this book, you will find observations, case studies, analysis, strategy, and tactics in the following five chapters:

Chapter 1 – To Hack Growth, Brands Have to Hack Culture First

The idea of "hacking" culture is a play on the concept of growth hacking, popular among the Silicon Valley startups that we use to point out that success of ideas, brands, and products predominantly depends on the mood of the times. There are two ways to hack culture. First is to root a brand in a subculture or a niche. Second is capturing the zeitgeist, or kuuki wo yomu, a Japanese word used to depict reading the atmosphere. In this chapter, you will find four ways to detect and successfully capitalize on the mood in culture: contradictions, coincidences, inversions, and oddities in the culture, society, business, and consumer behavior.

Chapter 2 – Three Models of Social Influence

Thanks to platforms like Instagram and TikTok, consumer choice across categories is now more susceptible to social influence than to individual preferences. But how we influence each other is unpredictable. No amount of celebrity is going to make popular a product that no one wants. At the same time, we seek ideas and trends that capture their imagination, conversations, and a cultural moment. To explain how to make success of products, services, and ideas less random, in this chapter, you will learn about the three models of social influence: the two-step flow of communication (popularized by Malcolm Gladwell's book The Tipping Point); the model called "accidental influentials" that explains success of Marie Kondo, Dollar Shave Club, and "ok boomer"; and algorithmic personalization where platforms like TikTok, Instagram, Netflix, and Spotify themselves create popular trends, ideas, and aesthetics.

Chapter 3 – Why Taste Communities Are the Future of Marketing

We are going through the imagined community renaissance, thanks to modern brands stepping in as the social constructs of belonging left vacant by traditional institutions of social cohesion, like organized religion, civil society institutions, and mass media. Consumer collectives are the new audience unit. In this chapter, I suggest that, instead of focusing on individuals, brand professionals should look at the communities these individuals belong to. When we shift our focus from an individual to their network of relationships, we start asking different questions: how the communities an individual belongs to are structured; what is their dynamics; how the influence spreads within them; who are the most active and/or valuable members. This shift reveals not our inferred, but our actual taste. Netflix's taste communities are a variation of this idea. Its 125 million global viewers are divided into 2,000 "taste clusters" that group people based on their movie and TV show preferences. Thanks to its banks of data, Netflix goes beyond the psychographics of its average customer. Applied to the world of physical objects, this approach transforms how trends, things, and ideas are created, bought, and sold. In this chapter, you will learn about what how consumer niches create and spread taste, how to target consumer collectives, and what are fan-made brands, created by imagined communities of fans that do not necessarily know each other but share tastes, aesthetics, and interests.

Chapter 4 – Mimicry as Taste: Why Cultural Sameness Is a Matter of Social Design

The modern aspiration economy is filled with examples of products, services, and brands that are popular because they are sharable social symbols: MSCHF, Instagram Face, Baby Yoda, Rimowa luggage, matching pajama sets, minimalism, intermittent fasting, Peloton. Thanks to the Internet, products across categories are now more susceptible to trends than to individual preferences. It's easy to blame algorithms for the sameness of our taste choices, but the real culprit is us. Humans use social signals to quickly orient themselves in the world. On a daily basis, we actively classify one another by lifestyle, values, interests, and projected and perceived social standing. Based on taste displays, people make snap decisions of whether a person is like them or far away in taste space, and thus foreign. Just like crickets or light bulbs, albeit amplified with Instagram likes, Twitter hashtags, and other performance metrics, our taste signals get harmonized, so all of us end up looking the same, dressing the same, liking the same things, and visiting the same places. In addition to being a great mechanism in learning how to orient, belong, and present oneself in the world, imitation is responsible for social cohesion. In this chapter, you will find specific examples from the modern aspiration economy (coffee shops design, Airbnb aesthetics, Instagram "look") to analyze how social classification and social cohesion move culture toward the world that's harmonized and homogenous in taste.

Chapter 5 – The 4Cs: Brand Strategy Meets Aspiration Economy
At the time of Veblen, brand strategy was simple: marketers aimed their communication at targets defined by their household income and purchasing habits and their messages encouraged consumption of commodities as a way to accrue status. Now they have the opportunity to flip the script by focusing on one or more of the 4Cs: content, community, collaborations, and curation. In this chapter, you will find success stories from each of the four pillars and explanation of why and how they modernize culture, society, and businesses.

Bibliography

Currid-Halkett, Eli, *The Sum of Small Things: A Theory of the Aspirational Class*, Princeton: Princeton University Press, 2017.
Eckhardt, G., "The New Dynamics of Status and Distinction," *Marketing Theory* 20(1): 85–102, 2020.

To hack growth, brands have to hack culture first

1

The idea of "hacking" culture is a play on the concept of growth hacking popular among the Silicon Valley startups that we use to point out that success of ideas, brands, and products predominantly depends on the mood of the times. There are two ways to hack culture. First is to root a brand in a subculture or a niche. Second is capturing the zeitgeist, or *kuuki wo yomu*, a Japanese word used to depict reading the atmosphere. In this chapter, you will find four ways to detect and successfully capitalize on the mood in culture: contradictions, coincidences, inversions, and oddities in the culture; society; business; and consumer behavior.

In early April of 2020, more than 20,000 people signed a petition to name Dr. Anthony Fauci the "Sexiest Man Alive." The honor is bestowed annually by *People* magazine, and past honorees include Hollywood stars, musicians, and celebrities like John Legend, George Clooney, Brad Pitt, and The Rock. Dr. Fauci is the director of the National Institute of Allergy and Infectious Diseases.

In those days, our heroes were carers and healers: nurses, doctors, drivers, cleaners, postal workers. The invisible, underpaid, taken-for-granted, they came together to protect us from the pandemic. In her Easter speech, the Queen of England expressed her hope that "in the years to come, everyone will be able to take pride in how they responded to this challenge."

Tell that to fashion influencer and proto-blogger Arielle Charnas.

We were unprepared for this crisis because our national heroes are soldiers and warriors. Our social heroes are nuclear scientists and tech inventors. Our cultural heroes are influencers and celebrities.

In the past several decades, we moved from "we" to "I": to Silicon Valley visionaries to Avengers to cult personalities of self-actualization, focused on getting, not giving. "We get one life, so why not milk the shit out of it?" asks Gwyneth Palthrow in her GOOP Netflix trailer.

Our worldly success outbids our desire to be a good person, resulting in fraying of the social fabric of our communities and demise of the traditional institutions that held them together. We put radical individualism ahead of society, and ignored the secondary effects of our choices. This wasn't hard to do: climate change was something that happened in the future and far away (until it didn't) and a deadly virus was invisible and foreign (until it wasn't).

Our job is to make the secondary effects of our choices – what our individual actions do to our communal ties and our environment – visible. Making these further-out effects visible will force us to take them into account.

"If men define situations as real, they are real in their consequences," says the Thomas theorem. There never was a better time to interpret this deadly global pandemic as an opportunity to reorganize our communities around new influencers, aspirations, social rituals, and habits.

New heroes

"We will succeed," promised the Queen. "This time we join all nations across the globe in common endeavor. Using the great advances of science and our instinctive compassion to heal, we will succeed, and that success will belong to every one of us." To the Queen and to David Bowie, we can all be heroes, because our individual decisions matter. They impact our self-perception and the way we present ourselves in our interactions. The way we socially label ourselves becomes, in the self-fulfilling prophecy, part of our identity. Our individual decisions also impact others. If we self-quarantine, our neighbors are more likely to do the same. If we wear a protective face mask in the supermarket, we set the example for others. If we stand two meters apart, we signal the necessity of social distancing.

There has been a lot of talk about how social media influencers and celebrities are behaving in this crisis: do we want to hear from them, do we not want to hear from them, and if we hear from them, what they should say? Consensus seems to be, the less, the better. We are not looking for travel inspiration and don't suffer from FOMO. We are looking for a kindred spirit, shared circumstances, realness.

When it comes to realness, we are looking up to people who are at its forefront. An emergency room physician Darien Sutton is on Instagram, where he shares public health measures and occasionally (and rightfully) calls out irresponsible social media influencers. There are more like him: we now gather around medical influencers, nurse influencers, but also home exercise influencers, meditation influencers, baking influencers.

People also approve of brands and establishments that turn to positive social action. Eleven Madison in New York reopened as a communal kitchen that serves nearly 3,000 meals a day to doctors, nurses, and essential workers throughout the city. Some raise a pint virtually for local bars; others turn their car dealerships into a delivery fleet, or their hotel rooms to medical staff, like Hilton did in partnership with American Express.

Right now, we turned our attention away from brands and influencers promoting consumption toward our own socially responsible behavior and to those enacting social cohesion, responsibility, and compassion. This is a good thing. It expands the playing field of whom and what we want to identify with, and aspire to be and do. It also reorganizes our communities under different personality cults: more generous, prosocial, and giving.

Cult objects

"The city was one's dining room, living room, and extended home - rather than the apartment, which is just where we went to sleep at night," writes Elizabeth Currid-Halkett in her book *The Sum of Small Things*. Even for 2017, when this book was published, this view feels dated: it's somehow closer to the "Sex and The City" era than to anyone's actual behavior. Some years before "Coronavirus and The City," young people came to the conclusion that going out requires "too much effort," according to the 2018 Mintel report. Instead, they started to invest in plants, cookware, meditation cushions and decorative pillows, candles, and bath bombs. "The Great Indoors" is the title of 2017 sense article, which captured emerging trends like hygge, baths, and spending more time in one's home. In 2019, author and consultant's Venkatesh Rao term "domestic cozy" was officially elevated to the level of a coveted lifestyle.

Forget the latest Fendi bag, today's cult objects are pajamas, home leisure, sourdough bread, a Peloton bike, a yoga mat, a collection of plants. We have already carefully weaved these objects into our social routines and taste regimes, as reflected in the boom of magazines and brands that revere the ordinary and the everyday. "This is the stuff life is made of: sparks of beautiful, ordinary hope," writes Ruby Tandoh in her April 15, 2020, Eater essay titled "Finding Food Pleasures in a Time of Crisis."

Today, focus on the ordinary is a matter of survival. By staying at home, we prevent the virus from spreading and thus protect others. By focusing on the everyday, we keep ourselves sane.

Habits become institutions, per sociologists Peter Berger and Thomas Luckmann. Any action that's repeated frequently "becomes cast into a pattern." Our daily rhythms in isolation – cooking, exercising, working, decorating, celebrating holidays, and even mourning – become rituals of social cohesion. When coronavirus made our social structures collapse, rituals of domesticity is all we'd got.

Consequences are far-reaching. Institutionalized domesticity impacts economy, as it shapes our spending and leisure. Institutionalized social distancing impacts much more. Direct economy – in food, hospitality, entertainment, and culture – emerged from the forced lack of direct social contact, and is bound to stay. On April 6, Quartz reported that Chinese consumers have cut spending on "trivial things." One of the things that were cut is buying coffee in coffee shops, and instead making it at home. As spending and leisure patterns rearrange themselves, so will the consumer economy. Brands should pay attention to what consumers are doing right now – how they organize their days through rituals and daily rhythms – to get a glimpse of their future behavior.

Days of glory

A social script is the preestablished pattern of behavior that people are expected to follow in specific social situations. Right now, most of our social scripts have been torn apart: we cannot greet each other, celebrate, grieve and bury our dead, or sit by the bedside of our sick.

At the same time, the new social scripts are being formed: checking in on the elderly people and the vulnerable, volunteering, having a better hygiene, being comfortable with telemedicine, working from home, taking care of the homeless. Micro-changes in everyday life are influenced by macro-changes (like this pandemic). Vice versa is also true, and our instinct to imitate and conform changes of both our behavior and the way we view the world is a powerful tool towards more generous, responsible, and compassionate social scripts.

The new narratives are already emerging: the *Gruffalo* author Julia Donaldson drew her characters socially distancing and helping the vulnerable with their shopping. Culture is ready to gather (virtually) and entertain: TikTok is hosting a free 48-hour livestream festival, and a big number of outlets, from theaters to opera to clubs, are streaming their content directly.

Brands, en masse, started to put forward stories of collective capacity for action and duty to care (for example, see Dove Beauty's spring 2020 campaign, "Courage is Beautiful," which depicts male and female nurses and physicians with scars from protective face masks.). By their very nature, brands are uniquely positioned to carry these new narratives out. At the moment, radical individualism is out, social connection is in. Brand focus is not on the end customer, but on the communities they belong to. Just as personas made individual consumers visible, the new brand methodology makes visible consumer communities and their co-dependencies and influences. New focus of engagement plans is not just on the brand actions but on their secondary effects. Pre-pandemic consumer-centric brand strategy is now society-centric strategy.

In the past month, the Western culture has, out of necessity, become more "we" than "I" (with the wellness industry caught in crosshairs). The Queen asked us to put our moral selves ahead of our economic selves. There is a clear aspiration to have a more robust health system and public service, more collective-oriented and equal society, and to course-correct political agendas.

In the meantime, there's pop culture. Our dress, memes, aesthetic, and language are changing, and not only because of *Tiger King*. Kanye, ever the innovator, seems to have already adopted the hospital gear aesthetic in the form of his Season 8 boot. Face masks have been hailed as new sneakers, and indeed, streetwear face mask market is lit.

If our lexicon has been full of military metaphors ("take a stab at something," "attack a problem"), maybe now it will get replaced with the nursing, caring, and healing metaphors. "It took a nuclear disaster to get me to do it," said one food wholesaler in the middle of the deadly global pandemic to describe his business pivot. We still use phrases like "nuclear" and "WWIII" and root for lone heroes out on mission impossible 19 to save the world.

This crisis is finally forcing us to consider communal heroes, and to celebrate ordinary people who distinguish themselves by going against their social instinct to benefit the community. Hard-won experience, intelligence, and competence are all of a sudden sexy. It better be: what we do now will be evaluated by Greta Thunberg's generation, and the generations that follow. The value we put forward now are the values that future will rest on.

Brands need to pay attention to who, what, and how consumers celebrate in the modern world. Even before the crisis, and in the relatively stable time of mass media, success of a brand campaign, initiative, or a collaboration was unpredictable. "Half the money I spend on advertising is wasted; the trouble is, I don't know which half," a famous advertising industry adage goes.

Thanks to Instagram, YouTube, Snapchat, and Pinterest, we are more than ever exposed to one another's decisions when it comes to what to buy, wear, and like. We are susceptible to peer pressure and social influence, and this human tendency makes unpredictability higher than ever.

Case in point: Glossier is today one of the most successful beauty companies around. At one point, there were 10,000 people on a waitlist just for its lipstick. But before founder Emily Weiss landed $52 million in Series C funding, no one predicted anything like Glossier. In fact, 11 investors had turned Weiss down.

When it comes to cultural products like food, fashion, design, or travel, things that worked in the past often do not work in the present (the sheer number of *The Avengers* sequels notwithstanding). But despite the inherent unpredictability of consumer tastes and the complex way they interact, Venture Capitalists (VC) still put a heavy bet on pattern recognition. These patterns – be it a proprietary product, low-cost customer acquisition tactics, or the ability to reach scale fast – are hardly reliable predictors of success.

Glossier succeeded because it recognized that women enjoy sharing their beauty preferences, it and gave them the tools to create content that enabled conversations around it. Glossier's value is not in the sheer scale of its user base, but rather in the interactions within it.

Consider the following example. Grooming company Harry's proprietary razors, manufactured in its German factory, were a great initial way for the brand to differentiate itself from Gillette's low-quality but expensive razors. But superior product quality has since become table stakes in the shaving market, with a number of startups all offering the same key features. Five years and 375 million VC dollars later, Harry's has only 5% market share in the traditional retail sales market and is a distant third in the online manual shave market. Not until Walmart (ironically, the retailer that Harry's DTC model set out to disrupt) provided its massive distribution muscle did Harry's business start to shift. To stay competitive in this mass market, Harry's now needs to worry about shelf space and brand marketing – just like Gillette.

Dollar Shave Club, with 21% of the online market share, was not profitable when Unilever bought it in 2016. Its VC-beloved debut online video was viewed more than 25 million times since 2012. Social media quickly made a lot of people know of Dollar Shave Club but also undid its staying power. The main lesson is that wide awareness doesn't mean conversion and that seeing the fast user growth doesn't mean profitability. To hack growth, startups have to "hack" culture first.

The dynamics of how trends are created and how they spread shifted from brands, media, and retailers pushing ideas to mass market, to the Internet networks of niches and taste communities. This shift forces brands to consider social processes that ultimately define the success of their products and services. There are two approaches to "hacking culture."

The first one is for a brand to find a subculture or a niche and grow from there. This is the strategy employed by outdoor activewear brand Patagonia. Patagonia connected early with the hardcore climbing community and the love of nature, environmentalism and sustainability that this community shares with the brand. Subculture of outdoor enthusiasts is made of people who are more passionate about being outdoors than about anything else. They are likely to be beta testers, source material, and advocates for a new product, service, or message. A deep subculture entrenchment ensures that a company can maintain and enhance its difference as it scales. Patagonia's long-term brand defensibility has more to do with it being able to believably connect with its community through the shared passion than if it had a proprietary product or acquisition channels.

The second one is for a brand to capitalize on the culture of social responsibility. Japanese have a great expression, *kuuki wo yomu*, which translates as "reading the atmosphere." Products, brands, and ideas are more likely to succeed if consumers are already susceptible to them and are easily persuaded to invest their time and money in them. For example, in the October 2013 article titled "Yes, Real Men Drink Beer and Use Skin Moisturizer," Bloomberg magazine quotes Mintel's data on the five-year rise in the global sales of personal-care merchandise geared for men. Harry's was founded earlier that year, Dollar Shave Club two years prior. Both of them capitalized on the shift in the culture of modern masculinity, but neither of them invented it. Men were already thinking about grooming differently. As sociologist Duncan Watts notes in his research on social influence (2007), if a society is ready to embrace a trend, almost anyone can start one – and if it isn't ready, then almost no one can. The success of Harry's or Dollar Shave Club didn't have to do much with a spiffy video or the German factory-produced razors. It had more to do with how susceptible men already were to the idea of grooming and how easily persuaded they were to invest in it. This example shows that the fastest way for a brand to engineer social influence is to piggyback on the already existing social influence and to amplify it through go-to-market strategy that emphasizes social activity among a company's initial following. This social activity serves as an ad for a product or service aimed at the mass audience. Running brand Tracksmith's initial community of runners – and their stories – became the ad for its products; interviews with members of fashion apparel's brand Doen community the ad for Doen's clothes.

Let's explore both in more detail.

Niches and subcultures

Rostro is a coffee shop near Yoyogi Park. Sit down at a bar, and you are faced with an option of different flavors (sweet, nutty, fruity, tart) and different strengths, depending on the grounds-to-water ratio. Make your selection, and you are in for a carefully choreographed ritual. It starts with hand-grinding the coffee beans with a device seemingly dating from the turn-of-the-last century that I last saw in my grandmother's house, followed by a lab-like system of syphon tubes. Each step is done with a lot of care, skill, and technique. The coffee, once it arrived, was great, as was the members-only feel surrounding it, but the nuances of its flavor and texture were lost on me. I am not a coffee connoisseur.

There are a lot of those who are. There are also foodies, audiophiles, vinyl lovers, fitness junkies, sneakerheads, fashionistas, soccer fans, global nomads, wellness aficionados. In each of these self-identified taste groups, taste is an activity that engages them on more than a casual level. Coffee, food, travel, and exercise are not passive leisure activities. Instead, they require investment of consumers' attention, time, and money. The more time, attention, money, and skill consumers spend on them, coffee-making, cooking, and traveling become more enjoyable. Specific techniques and rituals emerge. Community is formed. A vocabulary emerges ("beaters," "deadstock," "upotwns"). Those obsessed with their vinyl collections, sneakers, or fitness regimen can speak for hours about it.

In the modern aspiration economy, taste is not given. It's not a passive play of social differentiation. It's an activity that is continuously developed, cultivated, and refined.

It's an activity that includes objects (e.g. sneakers, coffee beans, food), other participants (e.g. sneakerheads, menswear forums, friends, a local coffee barista), specific ways of doing things (e.g. syphon or drip coffee, getting info on sneaker drops), written materials (e.g. reviews, magazines, Instagram), history (e.g. a specific tradition or role playing), tools and devices (e.g. cooking and fitness equipment), and attention and sensibilities (e.g. expanding one's wine or coffee or food palette).

All of these – objects, community, methodology, history, technique, and tools – increase, augment, and give feedback on taste. We develop our taste by absorbing social and cultural capital around us. For example, through its content, conversation, products, techniques, reviews, and um, devices, GOOP increased and refined our individual and collective sensibilities around self-care.

Historically, taste has been linked to aesthetics or class. For French sociologist Pierre Bourdieu, who wrote the book titled *Distinction*, social class determines creation and expression of taste ("nor quite our class, darling").

For Veblen, taste acts as a social barrier: upper class uses it to distance itself from the lower class. The moment that lower class adopts certain tastes, upper class abandons them and moves toward the new ones.

Both class determinism and social signaling are passive: a person is born into taste; a way of dress is a signal of social standing. Today's rental and resale economy upended all of that, but beyond the new accessibility of luxury and the new forms of capital, there's a bigger play here.

Taste is still a boundary-making mechanism (my unrefined coffee palette excludes me from having any coffee-related status) and is an engine of social difference. But it's an active one: were I to decide today to become a coffee junkie, I would start watching YouTube how-to videos, order a stack of coffee magazines, find online forums and offline communities, learn tricks, make a pilgrimage to an infinite number of kissatens, subscribe for an equipment, both syphon-based and drip-based, and start working on my skill, technique, and methodology. I would adopt a new social role and develop a ritual around my coffee-drinking. I'd train my sensibilities, perceptions, and palette. Very soon, I would be able to confidently order nutty-medium roast and to enjoy it, too.

Due to the serious investments of time and money and attention that I'd make in order to develop my competency and become well-versed in all things coffee, there's still a heavy social hierarchy surrounding taste. But taste is decoupled from class.

Instead, taste creates new social formats. The coffee culture – and all the spaces, rituals, communities, methods, and coffee-making instruments it contains – is one example. Niche magazines are another.

At the 2019 Magazine Innovation Center's annual conference, the future of magazine media was proclaimed to be "niche, specialized content produced with excellence." Indeed, like indie bookstores, niche magazines seem to be thriving.

There are magazines covering tennis, outdoor living in Canada, Jane Dickson in Times Square, modernist Detroit, food and art, mental health, craft beer, contemporary feminist witchcraft, cannabis, farming. These days, chances are that there's a magazine somewhere in the world that speaks directly to just about anyone's taste.

The Plant magazine is "a remarkable ode to botanical beauty." *A Dance Mag* comes from Beirut and aims to transcend cultural differences via dance. *Record* is a bi-annual publication for niche music communities. *Buffalo Zine* is a 400+ page book fusing food and fashion. MUNDIAL was initially launched as a one-off for celebrating Brazil's 2014 World Cup. Today, it's a magazine, a store, and a brand consultancy that's "a market leader in understanding modern football culture and how it affects brands, consumers, and fans around the world." Come in for a T-shirt, stay for a consulting gig.

What unites all of these magazines, regardless of the taste niche they cater to, is that they change consumers' relationship with the world. Taste fills products with meaning. "We wanted not just to be a provider of Japanese coffee equipment, but to focus on the education of the Japanese way of home brew, the Japanese coffee culture, and the art of coffee itself," says Yozo Otsuki, founder of the Japanese specialty coffee and artisan brewing equipment site Kurasu. These days, it's never just about coffee (or food, or wellness). It's about the art of living.

There are four ways that brands can capitalize on this

Start with empathy for a particular group of people and their particular tastes. A good number of niche magazine founders are part of their targeted audience, and they themselves recognized a gap in part of their lifestyle. The outcome is that readers feel like there's nothing out there like the niche magazine they subscribed to (and there probably isn't). It takes commercial magazines longer (if at all) to recreate this feel. Application for brands is to see if they can create or market or package a subgroup of products that caters to a targeted subgroup of their overall audience.

Introduce creative flexibility. Niche magazines have a lot more creative flexibility than commercial ones: they can change their font, cover art, features, and so forth from issue to issue. This creative flexibility generates iconic looks and differentiates them from commercial publications. Having a one-off magazine issue that doesn't look like any other one appeals to a collector's mentality and turns items into collectibles. Application for brands is to experiment with creative flexibility in a cost-effective way: to invest in limited-edition packaging, limited-edition colors or patterns, or one-off products that differentiate not only the brand from its competitors but the products within the same collection.

Create a taste regime. Niche magazines help consumers exercise their taste in their everyday life. They provide a framework – a set of tricks and hacks and reviews and tools and a community — to practice one's taste. *The Plant* magazine transforms one's home and one's self and creates rituals and routines that guide everyday action of caring for plants. Application for brands is to give consumers a framework for exercising their taste, either through an online magazine or blog or Instagram account; through events and partnerships; or through curation of best practices, mentors, and role models. The idea is to put forward content and events that influence how people relate with a brand's products and what they do with them.

Define taste communities. The production of taste makes its own collectives with a shared lifestyle, ways of dressing, speaking, diet and nutrition, spending time. (For example, see how Rothy's community developed around the shared consumer lifestyle: "it's more than a shoe, it's sisterhood.") In developing taste, the community is the necessary springboard: it includes mentors, role models, and reference points. Taste is a most efficient group-maker.

Kuuki wo yomu

At any point during the week in the pre-coronavirus time, a person could stop by Fort Defiance restaurant in the Red Hook neighborhood of Brooklyn, New York, to have an excellent cocktail, enjoy friendly atmosphere, and find reprieve after being snottily told by Red Hook Tavern that the wait is 1.5 hour, no matter when they showed up.

These days, Fort Defiance sells groceries. On their site, one can find butter, parsley, chicken drumsticks, raw honey, or bottled Negroni. There are also gift certificates. Across the Atlantic, UK milkmen are going through demand renaissance, although less of a farm-to-table and more of a shelter-in-place variety. Leon's chain of restaurants pivoted to selling pre-packaged meals available for pickup and delivery.

In New York, premium food wholesalers like Chef's Warehouse, F. Rozzo and Sons, or Happy Valley Meat Co. now sell their goods directly to consumers. Their specialty items once went to the likes of Gramercy Tavern and Eleven Madison. Today, Eleven Madison is a communal kitchen, and a person doesn't need to endure Frenchette's alarmingly bad acoustics in order to enjoy their food; they can have the same meat and produce in the quiet hum of their own home. At-home cooks are the winners here: they get access to luxury meat boxes and other goods at wholesale prices. They have nothing but time on their hands, and abundant inspiration and resources, with everyone from Michelin-star chefs like Massimo Bottura streaming cooking lessons, to cookware and food brands posting recipes at every opportunity.

Arguably, ghost kitchens got there first. According to the National Restaurant Association, a 60 percent of restaurant meals are now consumed off-premises. That was before the crisis, when being a homebody was still a generational thing and a lifestyle choice.

The current pivot to direct is different. As sometimes is the case with innovations, this one is born out of necessity. Industries were caught unawares before (analog photography, retail, newspapers) by "creative destruction" of technology. But innovation-by-necessity has little to do with any new technology. This is perhaps why we find it so confusing and its consequences so hard to grasp.

Chinese farmers from rural counties have been, for a while now, using livestreaming to hawk and sell their agricultural products to the urban residents. Alibaba got them to use its Taobao's livestreaming content and e-commerce capabilities as a way to revitalize countryside and lift small-scale agricultural producers out of poverty (in addition to expanding its content and audience market). When pandemic hit Wuhan, rural farmers selling their meats and vegetables directly to the city residents became a life-line for the quarantined.

We are better at explaining tech innovation when it transforms economy, society, and culture, than the other way around. We have plausible AI, blockchain, driverless cars, and commercial space flights scenarios. We are successful in "anticipating" things that are, in some form or to some degree, already happening. This is why we think of this crisis as a "great acceler-ator" of the future:

Earlier this year, Shanghai Fashion Week partnered with Tmall and was entirely livestreamed where designers and brands presented their upcoming collections directly, in the "see now, buy now" manner, to 800 million active users. Or, beauty brands Deciem and Kiehl's launched one-on-one digital consultations aimed at bringing their retail teams' expertise to consumers stuck at home. E-commerce marketplaces saw a 14 percent in a single week (March 23–30). Earlier in March, author Shea Serrano and writer Roxane Gay gathered a large sum in direct donations on Twitter for people facing financial hardship due to the pandemic.

But all of these changes were already under way before the pandemic: fashion week has long been in flux and designers were experimenting with livestreaming and see-now-buy-now formats. Beauty consumers have already been primed to expect one-on-one consultations. E-commerce has been rising steadily for some years now, and peer-to-peer giving is an already established lending format.

While not always linear, technological innovation is a directional pro-gression. We believe that it leads to a "better" or, at least, enhanced world, even in the doomsday scenarios. In sci-fi, popular culture, and Silicon Valley, when humans meet some horrible fate, it's usually because of good tech intentions gone awry. For example, when humans stumble upon hostile aliens, this is because they were exploring space; when they perish in an apocalypse, it's because they were perfecting their weaponry; when they get addicted to social media, it's because they strived to connect the world.

With tech innovation, bad things are a negative externality of good things. In contrast, innovation by necessity – social, economic, environmental – doesn't create side effects. It itself is a side effect (in this case, of a global pandemic). The future is a non-sequitur. One day, I was having Sunday lunch with my family; the next day my dad was drafted to counter-air defense to fight NATO planes (he's still among us).

We like the future that we can anticipate – but sometimes things that we can anticipate don't become the future. The culture industry is at the moment going direct. Under the "United We Stream" umbrella, a collaboration of 40 Berlin nightclubs livestream DJ sets every night, starting at 7 pm, directly into partygoers homes (at least that's a club that everyone can get in). At the beginning of the outbreak in New York City, Metropolitan Opera started nightly livestreaming of its past performances. Broadway plays and musicals switched to streaming. And on Saturday, on April 11, Brooklyn music venue, nightclub, and arts space Elsewhere will open in Minecraft. There are detailed instructions for how to listen to the audio stream and the hashtag, #NetherMeant, for sharing experience on Twitter; those who can't join the game, can still watch the Twitch stream.

Just like restaurants and fine food wholesalers, culture industry could have adopted any of the aforementioned scenarios before the pandemic; clubs could have streamed their music and MET their operas. But it didn't occur to anyone that this is a desirable human experience; no establishment proud of its name would dream of replacing the "real" thing with the virtual (this is perhaps why so many of us have been reluctant to embrace VR before this). Social experience is defined by setting, gestures, expressions, the vibe we give off, interaction rituals, moods, emotional signaling, and role playing, and it is rooted in our physicality. We are attention-seeking creatures, and when we go out, we "perform" for others, per sociologist Erving Goffman, and this performance gives "meaning to ourselves, to others, and to our situation."

Prime food wholesalers and restaurants are likely to keep their newfound business model after this crisis. After all, selling inventory directly to consumers, in addition to the bulk restaurant orders, doesn't add much in terms of cost and is an additional, albeit minor, source of revenue. That's not the point: having an opportunity to connect with new customers directly builds the wholesalers' brand awareness and equity and influences consumer decision-making.

Knowing where a restaurant's food comes from can become a legitimate dining choice, in the vein of "let's have Natoora's truffles tonight, see which restaurant serves them." The fragility of this behavior is also obvious: if consumers can buy truffles directly from a Michelin-star restaurant supplier and if they can have a Michelin-star chef's cooking tutorial livestreamed, they may opt out of going to restaurants altogether – unless the restaurants pivot again, this time away from serving, and toward music and entertainment, design, theater, grocery, and extreme displays of food-preparing skills.

Just like Bilibili, Weibo, Taobao, or Lizhi revenue streams are increasingly less dependent on advertising (unlike their US counterparts) and increasingly diversified to include virtual gifts, e-commerce, livestreaming, and subscriptions, industries across the board will have to socially, economically, and environmentally diversify to position themselves for the post-pandemic future.

Why we have such a hard time to make *kuuki wo yomu* work for us

In the spring of 2020, it was very popular to call the coronavirus crisis a great accelerator. True as it may be, I find non-tech, innovation-by-necessity pivots a more fertile analytical soil.

Brands like olive oil producer Brightland pivoted to content, community, and curation with the same ease and care, and with the same mission that it used to sell its olive oil. Aperitif brand Haus promptly put its unique market position (being exempt from alcohol laws) and its unique value chain (owning supply and production) to good use, by partnering with hard-hit restaurants to create signature aperitifs and sell them at 100 percent profit for restaurants. Once the hair salon he was working at closed on March 15, my hairdresser, Marshall Lin, immediately pivoted to creating content and sharing his hair care expertise online. Soon, he relaunched his website.

Examples are many, and should be celebrated as fervently as tech-fueled acceleration toward digital fashion week, e-commerce, online education, remote work, and so forth. All of these accelerations expose trends that have already been happening; to really learn, look into the unexpected and the different. Show me what's NOT accelerating and let's figure out why.

For example, when interacting with their coronavirus-infected patients, doctors and nurses wear protective gear at all times, with nothing but eyes visible. So they started to pin photos of themselves smiling on their hospital gowns, so their patients could see their faces and their smiles. This heartbreaking innovation is as good as Netflix Party. It also begets the question: now that we are all required to wear face masks in public, what will be our common gestures of meeting when we can't see each other's smiles? Smile has been a prominent feature of modern life since the middle ages (strangely enough, it wasn't "invented" until then).

Real generosity toward the future lies in giving it all to the present, said Albert Camus. The future is hidden in our present: in what we value, who we gather around and pay attention to, what we support, and what we rally against. The real challenge for marketers is to detect this mood while it is happening. To answer the question of how to get something to resonate with the atmosphere of the times, we should look for contradictions, inversions, oddities, and coincidences in our culture, society, and economy. Originally coined by futurist Paul Saffo (2012), contradictions, inversions, oddities, and coincidences are indicators that change is ahead.

Contradictions happen when two irreconcilable things coexist. In February 2020, the ordeal of Diamond Princess' passengers read like a horror story of the "this happens to other people" variety. One would think that its aftermath would wean not only cruise-lovers but also cruise-curious from setting a foot on a boat again. One would think.

Instead, during late March and April (the peak of the pandemic in the United States), there has been a 40 percent increase in 2021 cruise bookings on CruiseCompete.com compared to its 2019 bookings, reports Business Insider. Additionally, 76 percent of the travelers who canceled a cruise in 2020 chose to take credit toward a future cruise in 2021, compared to 24 percent who opted for a refund.

Consumer behavior changes infinitely less than prophets of all stripes predict right now. While it may take a bit for consumers to go back to their spending habits, brands should trust the muscle memory of spending and should not expect a radically changed consumer.

Or, outside the pandemic, the most visible cultural contradiction maybe is the simultaneous presence of cultural niches and the monoculture. On the one hand, across industries, we have content streaming, fragmentation of interests, and rise of niche products. There's a lament that our world is becoming a fragmented collection of tribes and fervent fandoms of *otakus*: a Japanese term for people with obsessive, laser-like interests. On the other hand, there's the existential dread of aesthetic gentrification in the form of Instagram Face, Airspace, Airbnb Style, and cultural homogenization. Consumers want choice, but in order to navigate it, they rely on others and so end up enjoying the same fashion trends, movies, diets, and songs. Mimicry and imitation are the decentralized mechanism of cultural production and social cohesion. Brands have to offer consumers choice but also use social signals to steer it.

Inversions are novel reversals in a trend dynamic. Today's relationship between conspicuous consumption and wealth is one such reversal. Less affluent individuals tend to acquire products that make them more socially visible and devote a higher share of their total spending to conspicuous consumption than the rich, who prefer to spend more discreetly and are less drawn to obvious status symbols, opting in for subtle signals of status, wellness, and inner transformation instead. Brands targeting high-net-worth individuals need to reposition around work-of-the-human-hands artistry and excellence versus the wannabe-rich, in-your-face communication codes.

In the spring of 2020, the inversion that aspiration has been going through reached its fever pitch. What was once aspirational – cooking, decorating, cocktail mixing, plant caring, at-home exercise – became commonplace. If we scrolled down our Instagram feed at the time, influencers' photos were the same as ours: we are all at home, baking sourdough bread, arranging flowers, and taking photos in our old outfits in the rooms and hallways. True, some were nicer than others, but the FOMO is gone. The Great Indoors and Domestic Cozy were aspirational as long as they were a matter of choice. They became mandatory and real (and not even of the "aspirational realness," but of the "real realness" quality). Everyone can have them.

In the inversion of aspiration, influencers were caught in crosshairs. If they behaved like everyone else, they were everyone else; if they behaved differently, they were called out for it. This scrutiny is new: before the pandemic, we were happy to indulge in the (relatively) harmless escapism that influencers provided. As long as we viewed influencers as predominantly commercial tools (no one really makes a mistake of considering these people real), we were happy for them to promote moon juice and poop tea. But the moment they revealed themselves as members of the society, we turned on them: not only because their wide reach spreads their socially irresponsible behavior further, but because without their commercial role, they are the same as us and therefore subject to the same rules.

There were also a number of inversions in our social rituals, and this led to change in the meaning of metaphors. "To give someone a wide berth" signaled steering clear of trouble and/or any social association with a person. In April 2020, it became a sign of socially responsible and respectable behavior.

Oddities are out-of-ordinary occurrences that make us search beneath the surface or a trend or pattern. There are currently a number of Internet communities that are part social club and part marketplace. They emerge around specific brands (e.g. Supreme, MSCHF, Peloton) or around shared values and interests of its members (e.g. sustainability, cultural memes, exercising). They are settings for bonding, sharing advice, and shopping for people who do not know each other, but who use their common interests, beliefs, and tastes to link up. These multi-purpose "imagined communities" are an alternative to the purely commercial retail models, as they enforce social interactions as much as product transactions. The task for modern brands is to appeal to both social and individual dimensions of consumption.

The biggest oddity during coronavirus pandemic was that our social isolation was the expression of social solidarity. Social cohesion was ensured by us staying apart. In all other times of crisis – wars, natural disasters, economic hardships – we were physically in them together. We gathered to alleviate the stress of the crisis, to emotionally support each other, to share stories, to help each other, and to enforce our social bonds. Not this time. In this crisis, we were together by being apart.

This oddity was also reflected in our new heroes: Dr. Anthony Fauci was petitioned to be named the Sexiest Man Alive; nurses, doctors, drivers, cleaners, postal workers grace covers of mainstream magazines and are profiled in advertising commercials. Communal heroes were in: ordinary people who do their duty and communities who gather to protect their vulnerable. We were looking up to those with knowledge, hard-won experience, honesty, responsibility, and competence.

Coincidences are about simultaneous appearance of distant and unrelated trends or patterns. Prior to the pandemic, if I found myself in an Airbnb in Europe or Asia, no matter where, there was a good chance there will be a photo of my red-brick Dumbo apartment building to welcome me. The resulting experience is known and new; diverse and familiar; authentic and recognizable; unique and replicable; wabi-sabi and polished. Technology, through the immediate social feedback loops, brings those disparate tendencies together. Recognizable and accessible cultural reference points, like Supreme, the Dumbo neighborhood, or Baby Yoda, work best here.

Coronavirus pandemic also exposed a number of coincidences. For example, in his Twitter thread from April 4, 2020, author and consultant Venkatesh Rao noted that, with regard to the coronavirus crisis, "Everything sweet and life-affirming in the business response is a feel-good ineffectual favela chic hope punk sideshow theater. Everything substantively driving the main act is grim dark gothic high-tech extractive profiteering by cartoon cultural capitalist ops." Rao went on to give examples of homemade face masks coinciding with bidding wars over protective equipment among states and hospitals, and photos of exhausted nurses coinciding with private equity firms behind hospitals calculating their bailouts.

These coincidences reveal the Big Split between the social organization and the economic system that underpins it. We are in the rare moment when two opposing forces – solidarity, community care – visibly coincide with opportunism, free riders, profiteering within the same structure. Volunteering and individual donations are at their peak; so is medical equipment piracy, and the federal government's failure to effectively protect small businesses and recently unemployed individuals. The structure cannot support these coincidences, and it will either reorganize itself or break. IMF warned of the expected social unrest around the globe, and Bloomberg recently reported on potential social revolutions. It is also likely that taxpayer money will be funneled toward making healthcare systems more robust and social security higher. Brands will have to find a way to deftly convey their simultaneous pro-social and pro-economic stance in their behavior and communication actions. Doing tangible good will have to become as rigorous and measurable goal as the business performance.

There are four implications for brands

Engineer social influence in your market. In addition to engineering products and services, brands need to engineer social influence in their market. The fastest way is to piggyback on already-existing social influence and amplify it through a go-to-market strategy that emphasizes social activity among a company's initial following. This social activity then serves as an ad for a product or service aimed at the mass audience. For example, luggage brand Away's initial community of travelers – and their stories – became the ad for its products; rides of the Rapha's Cycling Clubs are the ad for Rapha's gear.

Make social currency an inherent part of your business plan. Social activity in a market accumulates social capital. How a social currency is going to be created and exchanged should be an inherent part of business plan. It's a business' core value unit, and whether a company has the potential to build and trade in social currency should become part of VCs evaluative criteria. Beauty brand Glossier's currency is the beauty preferences of its fans. Glossier's currency is so strong that this brand is now creating the entire marketplace around it. Social currency builds scale, defensibility, and network effects.

Avoid reverse network effects. To prevent social currency from being devalued due to reverse network effects, companies need to maintain and grow their distinction as they scale. The best way to do this is through product and service diversification. A brand is an umbrella for a portfolio of unique products. The streetwear brand Supreme mastered the art of distinction, with a large part of its audience owning unique brand products and a limited number of people who own the exact same thing. Product diversification increases the number of bets, reduces risk, preserves social currency, and organizes a company around the inherent unpredictability of people's tastes.

Bibliography

Saffo, Paul, "8 Visionaries on How They Spot the Future," Wired, April 24, 2012, https://www.wired.com/2012/04/ff-spotfuture-qas/

Watts, Duncan J., "Is Justin Timberlake a Product of Cumulative Advantage?" New York Times, April 15, 2007, https://www.nytimes.com/2007/04/15/magazine/15wwlnidealab.t.html

https://www.change.org/p/people-magazine-make-dr-anthony-fauci-people-magazine-s-sexiest-man-alive/sign?original_footer_petition_id=18349899&algorithm=promoted&source_location=petition_footer&grid_position=10&pt=AVBldGl0aW9uAJsaQwEAAAAAXoPrfoJf+wxhOTIwZjAyOA==

https://arstechnica.com/gaming/2020/01/goops-netflix-trailer-paltrow-sinks-into-a-vagina-spews-pseudoscience/

https://www.nytimes.com/2020/04/02/style/influencers-leave-new-york-coronavirus.html

https://www.vanityfair.com/style/2020/04/influencers-coronavirus-arielle-charnas-escape-new-york

https://en.wikipedia.org/wiki/Thomas_theorem

https://www.nytimes.com/2020/03/30/arts/virus-celebrities.html

https://www.instagram.com/doctor.darien/?hl=en

https://www.adweek.com/digital/a-british-magazine-replaced-its-usual-celeb-cover-stars-with-medical-heroes/

https://www.today.com/style/dove-s-courage-beautiful-ad-honors-medical-workers-during-coronavirus-t178272

https://ny.eater.com/2020/4/2/21203434/eleven-madison-park-food-nonprofit-coronavirus-nyc

https://www.covidinnovations.com/home/11042020/molson-coor-company-launches-virtual-happy-hours-to-support-local-bars-and-restaurants-in-canada

https://www.covidinnovations.com/home/10042020/ibercaja-foundation-and-red-cross-launch-yocedomicoche-turning-car-dealerships-into-delivery-fleets

https://www.businesstraveller.com/business-travel/2020/04/06/hilton-and-american-express-donate-one-million-us-rooms-to-medical-staff/

https://www.mintel.com/press-centre/food-and-drink/the-stay-at-home-generation-28-of-younger-millennials-drink-at-home-because-it-takes-too-much-effort-to-go-out?utm_campaign=9543515_PR%2520US%2520Alcohol%2520Trends%2520release&utm_medium=email&utm_source=dotm&dm_i=2174,5OJTN,PXETVF,M3XYG,1

https://www.ssense.com/en-us/editorial/fashion/the-great-indoors

https://www.ribbonfarm.com/series/domestic-cozy/

https://www.instagram.com/and_premium/

https://brightland.co/
https://jingdaily.com/weve-had-athleisure-is-homeleisure-chinas-next-big-thing/
https://london.eater.com/2020/4/15/21221979/coronavirus-lockdown-food-comforts-eating
https://www.amazon.com/Social-Construction-Reality-Sociology-Knowledge/dp/0385058985
https://qz.com/1830777/china-consumers-wary-of-spending-after-coronavirus/
https://www.bbc.com/news/entertainment-arts-52149055
https://www.refinery29.com/en-us/2020/04/9684655/tiktok-music-lives-virtual-festival-live-stream
https://www.glamour.com/story/dove-courage-is-beautiful-campaign-healthcare-workers
https://www.nytimes.com/2020/04/08/style/wellness-self-care-coronavirus.html
https://www.highsnobiety.com/p/kanye-west-yeezy-season-8-boot/
https://mymodernmet.com/coronavirus-provider-photos-on-ppe/?utm_source=email&utm_medium=link&utm_campaign=newsletter&utm_term=2020-04-15
https://www.amazon.com/Distinction-Routledge-Classics-Pierre-Bourdieu/dp/0415567882/ref=sr_1_1?keywords=distinction&qid=1583864092&sr=8-1
https://racquetmag.com/
https://anxymag.com/
https://www.canamagazine.com/
www.sabatmagazine.com/
theplantmagazine.com/
www.adancemag.com/
https://record-magazine.com/
https://buffalozine.com/
https://mundialmag.com/
https://kurasu.kyoto/
https://www.vox.com/2020/1/13/21048371/rothys-shoes-flats-facebook-groups
https://andjelicaaa.substack.com/p/why-taste-communities-are-the-future
www.fortdefiancebrooklyn.com/new-products
www.fortdefiancebrooklyn.com/new-products/gift-certificate
https://www.standard.co.uk/business/restaurants-plan-to-be-minisupermarkets-in-bid-to-fix-food-shortages-and-catering-layoffs-a4390986.html
https://www.fastcompany.com/90487500/can-fine-dining-survive-covid-19-chef-daniel-humm-of-eleven-madison-park-isnt-so-sure
https://www.instagram.com/massimobottura/channel/
https://www.restaurant.org/Downloads/PDFs/Research/research_offpremises_201910

https://qz.com/quartzy/1748191/how-millennials-became-a-generation-of-homebodies/

https://www.investopedia.com/terms/c/creativedestruction.asp

https://jingdaily.com/how-digital-shanghai-fashion-week-will-affect-showrooms/

https://wwd.com/beauty-industry-news/beauty-features/beauty-inc-newsletter-beauty-retail-teams-gear-up-virtual-consultations-1203552367/

https://www.retaildive.com/news/prime-day-reportedly-postponed-until-at-least-august/575523/

https://www.nytimes.com/2020/03/16/business/coronavirus-bills-charity.html

https://www.nytimes.com/2020/03/17/theater/theater-streaming.html

https://elsewither.club/

https://www.twitch.tv/openpit

https://en.wikipedia.org/wiki/Erving_Goffman

https://brightland.co/blogs/field-notes

https://drink.haus/

https://drink.haus/pages/the-restaurant-project

www.linmarshall.com/

cruisecompete.com/

https://www.businessinsider.com/cruise-ship-bookings-are-increasing-for-2021-despite-coronavirus-2020-4

https://www.change.org/p/people-magazine-make-dr-anthony-fauci-people-magazine-s-sexiest-man-alive

https://abcnews.go.com/GMA/photos/people-magazines-sexiest-man-alive-years-12024905

https://time.com/collection/coronavirus-heroes/5816805/coronavirus-front-line-workers-issue/

https://twitter.com/vgr/status/1246588572976607232

https://nypost.com/2020/04/16/imf-warns-of-global-social-unrest-amid-coronavirus-pandemic/

https://www.bloomberg.com/opinion/articles/2020-04-11/coronavirus-this-pandemic-will-lead-to-social-revolutions

Three models of social influence   **2**

Thanks to platforms like Instagram and TikTok, consumer choice across categories is now more susceptible to social influence than to individual preferences. But how we influence each other is unpredictable. A celebrity is not going to make popular a product that no one wants. At the same time, we seek ideas and trends that capture their imagination, conversations, and a cultural moment. To explain how to make success of products, services, and ideas less random, in this chapter, you will learn about the three models of social influence: the two-step flow of communication (popularized by Malcolm Gladwell's book *The Tipping Point*); the model called "accidental influentials" that explains success of Marie Kondo, Dollar Shave Club, and "ok boomer"; and algorithmic personalization where platforms like TikTok, Instagram, Netflix, and Spotify themselves create popular trends, ideas, and aesthetics.

In the early spring of 2019, the most liked photo on Instagram was the picture of an egg named Eugene. With more than 53.9 million likes and 7.5 million followers, Eugene represented a mystery. The mystery of who created it and why has been since solved. How it got so many likes was best explained by a disgraced influencer, the model and actor Luka Sabbat: "People are way too influenced by what they see." Sabbat knows what he's talking about. Some months prior Eugene's debut, he was sued by his client, Snap, for his failure to exert influence. Similarly, Arii, an Instagram influencer with 2.8 million followers, could not sell a mere 36 T-shirts needed to start her own clothing line.

Social influence rests on the fact that, when faced with abundance of choice, we habitually rely on others to know what to buy, read, wear, or listen to. When these others are "regular" people just like us, we tend to trust them more than we would a compensated spokesperson, a model in an ad, an invisible editor, or a distant celebrity. Influencers are close and relatable, and we perceive their recommendations as "honest" and "authentic." Through our daily social media interactions, our vicarious presence at copiously documented weddings or births, we get to feel that we know our connections like we know our own friends.

But the social influence market is just like any market. It uses currency (taste) to build capital (social status). This capital eventually gets monetized, and we inevitably discover that our Internet "friends" may be making thousands and thousands of dollars for selling us brands, products, and ideas, just like celebrity pitch people did before them. A decade ago, the opposite of authentic influence was selling out; today, it's the reverse. Selling out equals being an authentic influencer, with a following and engagement large enough to be recognized and sought after by brands wanting to reach your audience. According to the research firm Neoreach, the number of Instagram posts using hashtags indicating advertising or promotion jumped from 1.1 million in 2016 to 3.1 million in 2018. And these are just the disclosed partnerships.

How we influence each other is unpredictable. No amount of celebrity (e.g. Luka Sabat) is going to make popular a product that no one wants. At the same time, we seek ideas and trends that capture their imagination, conversations and a cultural moment (e.g. egg Eugene). To make success of their products, services, and ideas less random, today's marketing practitioners settled on one of these three models of social influence.

The two-step flow of communication

For brand practitioners, the most prevalent model for thinking about social influence is still the two-step flow of communication. It was pioneered in 1950s by media theorists Elihu Katz and Paul Lazarsfeld (1955), and popularized by Malcolm Gladwell in his 2000 book *The Tipping Point*. The two-step flow of communication premise is that ideas, products, and trends depend on a few extraordinary people, such are Instagram stars, YouTube and TikTok creators, celebrities, and, most recently, grocery influencers. Today's $6.5 billion influencer marketing industry largely revolves around mega-influencers like these. Traditional cultural and industry gatekeepers – brands, editors, mass media, big influencers – wield less influencing power than that thought. As Arii's case revealed, one's audience doesn't translate into consumers and reach does not equal influence. Mega-influencers have reach, just like mass media. The best way for marketers to use them is for awareness, with cost per mille as the core metric, and to accept that they will not know which part of their budget is wasted.

The steady rise in social commerce only amplifies brands' quest for influencers. Powered by Instagram Checkout feature, social commerce means buying from people we follow, rather than going to actual stores and brand websites. Quite an oxymoron, social commerce represents the ultimate merger of money and influence, economy and culture, self-monetization and self-promotion. It turns consumption into creativity, and blurs the boundary between buying things and making things. It promises to create economic value while simultaneously making us feel socially valuable.

> The thing I find most exciting about social commerce is the potential it unlocks for creative entrepreneurs to get a leg up toward building legitimate businesses for themselves outside of traditional retail or wholesale methods. Some of the biggest brands in the world that are viewed as tremendously successful by most of the usual metrics still struggle with community-building or maintaining a legitimate connection with their customers.

Steve Dool, the head of Brand Partnerships, at the social commerce app Depop, told me.

> For people starting out to have platforms that not only enable that direct contact, but rely on it, can be extremely helpful for shaping inventory, brand identity, pricing—everything that defines their USP from the start, in real time. It's incredibly powerful to have that kind of connection, feedback and insights from Day 1, and can be liberating for people without the type of financial means to launch businesses with a big retail partner or a slick and pricey e-commerce site.

Instagram Checkout is part of a larger shift of the US social networks toward e-commerce. Chinese super apps like Little Red Book and WeChat's Good Product Circle have already turned Chinese collective review power into an integral part of their shopping experience. And, with the US platforms' ad models being under attack from regulators, adding social commerce capabilities is just a smart hedging strategy.

Retail tacticians are quick to celebrate all the wonderful things that the ultimate merger of inspiration and conversion will do to create an oft-missing link between performance and brand marketing and between awareness and sales.

Exciting as it may be, this tactical approach fails to see that social shopping means that platforms will bestow the same fate on retailers as they did on publishers. The platforms successfully monetized our attention. They are about to commercialize our social attachments. This will increase their power as gatekeepers, paralleled only by the regulatory confusion as to who pays the sales tax when we buy a product from an Instagram influencer.

Strategically, consequences of social commerce for branding, marketing, retailing, and socializing are as profound as they are unexplored. Here are some ways for brands to consider and implement social commerce.

Products over brands

Social commerce emphasizes individual taste and style savviness over brands: we are buying someone's look, not a particular brand within it.

> Younger shoppers in particular place premium on recommendations from peers over brands in terms of influencing purchasing decisions, another added benefit of allowing consumers to shop from people with similar interests and points of view, as opposed to brands that cater to their aesthetics or preferences.
>
> (notes Dool)

Marketing and promotional machinery will move toward product seeding across social shopping communities, monitoring the emerging best-sellers and amplifying the best performing product styling. This monitor-and-optimize, product-centric model is the opposite of brand-centric communication; it is also the opposite of the current influencer marketing model. In the social commerce context, products make influencers, not the other way around. Because this social dynamic varies per product and per its styling, permutations are as many as they are random and unpredictable. Social commerce gives a quick rise to new trends as much as it helps trends spread.

Taste bubbles

Instagram has recently been lauded as our "own personalized digital mall," ideally the only one we'd ever need. What a scary thought. Rise and dangers of content bubbles have already been copiously documented: across platforms, we repeatedly and increasingly see content that we already like, creating biases that can quickly scale. Now imagine a taste bubble, where we're served only things and styles and tastes that we liked in the past. A Google image search of the term "futuristic" shows what that may look like.

Longer product life cycles

If e-commerce took away the need to go to a physical store to browse, try on, and buy clothes, social commerce removes the need to permanently own them. The total resale market is expected to double in value to $51 billion in the next five years, according to a report from ThredUp. Traditional retail operates on product newness and seasonality. In contrast, social commerce extends product life cycle nearly indefinitely, as the same product can be resold and prosperously revived in many different styling iterations.

The great retail acceleration

On the social shopping app Depop, many popular looks are created, not by influencers but by "ordinary" people doing creative things with their clothes. Having many taste curators inevitably results in quicker trend cycles. People get bored and move onto the next look. Compressed zeitgeist, combined with extended product life, impacts retailers' operations, production, distribution, and merchandising strategy – all of which will have to become quick to respond to real-time, social data recording the ebbs and flows of our collective taste.

Everyone is direct-to-consumer

Today's trends are made by neither brands nor media. Social commerce puts this democratization of trend-making on steroids, as anything can be sold everywhere, by anyone, and to anyone. As Dool says:

> The Kylie Jenners of the world could probably set up a network of carrier pigeons and still turn a profit. I will say that I'm most interested in seeing how the social commerce element plays out on TikTok, which is introducing shoppable content earlier in its trajectory than so many other social platforms we've watched launch monetization efforts. I guess there's something very 2020 about buying stuff from someone who made their name dancing or jumping off the side of a building or whatever.

Social commerce is the most direct and immediate form of relationship between people and products, and it begets the question: if people now cultivate their own personalities in order to sell products and build a community, brands need to figure out what it is that they are doing. Originally created by companies to give selling a face and a human emotion, brands are getting killed by their own customers. People are increasingly more likely to build their own brand – and develop their own products, services, and experiences – than to endorse or be sponsored by someone else's.

Social commerce introduces new revenue streams, business models, marketing strategies, and regulatory hurdles. It also potentially turns us all into two-step communication broadcasters. Despite the lure of being an influencer, increasing number of Internet personalities and "regular" people alike opt to be curators instead.

Curators as influencers

In mid-2000s, a network theory scientist Duncan Watts introduced a model of social influence that he called "accidental influentials" (2007). Watts uses forest fire as an analogy to describe his model: if there's dry wood, lack of rain, density of trees, and remoteness of the fire department, any spark will cause a fire. It is a fertile social context, and not any particular influencer or a celebrity, that starts a trend. Ideas and products become popular because they capture the cultural moment and our imagination. Examples are the success of Harry's and Dollar Shave Club, astrology, Mari Kondo, cronuts, ok boomer, Greta Thunberg, meditation, going analog, hypebeasts. To create the right mood, some brands have been creating and managing the already existing conversations in subcultures, focusing on one small core user group and making their experience intimate, curated, and exceptional. The activity of this small user group is then used as owned media and widely spread. This approach has been adopted by Patagonia, Tracksmith, Rapha, and Glossier.

More recently, we are witnessing that curators are overtaking influencers as the core vehicle of capturing the cultural mood and starting trends. Consider the following example.

There's a bookstore in Ginza that sells only one book. "A single room with a single book" is its tagline. Every week, the owner chooses the book, presents it in the center of the shop, and curates an exhibition with artworks, photographs, or related items around its subject matter. Entering his bookstore is like entering a book.

In a less extreme scenario in the West, indie bookstores are thriving. The keyword is curation: by default, independent bookstores are local and community-oriented, and they get to know the taste of their regulars and the mood of the neighborhood.

Getting the taste and the mood makes indie bookstores a good model for the modern aspiration economy. Modern aspiration is not about having money to buy things, but having the taste to know what to buy. That's where human curation comes in, and why it's increasingly considered both a differentiator in fashion, food, travel, wellness, design, and an important value-add for tech platforms – from Spotify to Netflix and HBO, to Facebook and Apple.

Tsundoku is a Japanese word for the uncomfortable feeling of having too many books to read. It's also the MO of contemporary life. There are more than 75 startups looking to improve and streamline pet care. Industries as diverse as bedding, cookware, mattresses, makeup, fertility, apparel, dentistry, personal care, and so forth are all overflowing with options.

In this context, knowledge, judgment, and taste are valuable. We trust curators because we believe that they spent time and effort in developing their expertise. This belief seeped from the art world into the aspirational economy, with the new breed of aspirants looking to share their taste and turn their social and cultural capital into the economic one.

With a good reason, too: being a coveted curator of a cultural niche (e.g. menswear, streetwear, luxury fashion, design, food, or travel) conveys one's distinction and social standing based on more than posing on a cobblestone street in a selected outfit. It takes taste and knowledge to pick stuff up at Frieze in LA, Salone di Mobile in Milan, or Paris Fashion Week, as well as decide where to eat – in Berlin, Osaka, or Abu Dhabi.

Knowing where to go and what to do is the currency that, in the modern aspiration economy, makes curators more important than influencers. They guide their audience through culture by putting forward a selection of images, references, codes, product releases, or memes. Curation gives even mundane objects value by connecting them with a point of view, heritage, a subculture, or purpose that makes them stand out in the vortex of speed, superficiality, and newness.

Unlike influencers, curators often choose to remain anonymous as a way of boosting their cred. They are also not after the sheer reach and volume of followers: in their niches, it's the quality of followers that count. Hidden.NY is an anonymous curatorial account followed by Virgil Abloh and Drake. The mechanism through which curators shape culture is by becoming a source of inspiration for wider trends.

Making something part of a curated selection lets brands increase the price and the profit. A product's value is attached to the story. The Row's Instagram account is a careful selection of architecture, furniture, sculpture, and art, all of which convey an atmosphere. The idea is to present

The Row's clothes as just one expression of The Row's rarified taste and point of view.

For a brand (or a person) looking to become a curator, here are the four starting points:

Define what you're trying to accomplish (business objective). Decide what will curating achieve for you. For a brand, curation can retain an audience and attract the new one that hasn't considered a brand before. It can attract a collaborator or start a brand partnership. It can increase product value and protect pricing. For an individual, curation can be a way to get into a creative profession or monetize their taste.

Define the point of view and the story you're trying to tell (brand objective). Root your curation in one of the modes described later, and clearly define a filter that will distinguish things and behaviors that you focus on and those that you don't. Decide and specify what makes your curation distinct and what is the inimitable aspect of your own experience.

Define how you are going to convey this story in order to achieve your objective (strategy). Identify the sources of the material (products, videos, memes, references, images) for your curation. Define the subthemes or subcategories that enforce your wider narrative. Organize them according to your filter and clearly convey why they made the selection. Keep in mind that every item needs to tell the same story as the entire narrative.

Make an execution plan. Define the when and how often you will share, and how you'll socialize your selection and nurture your community. Decide who you'd like to attract.

There are a number of ways for brands to implement curation, and here are some of the mechanisms to select and organize items by:

Values. Filtering brands within a category based on their values (gender equality, sustainability, diversity) makes it easier to make a decision between products with similar properties. For example, The Helm is a platform that curates only products by brands with female founders, across categories. The Helm's tagline is "Make It Easy to Invest in Women," and, indeed, in the context where female founders command infinitely less VC money than men, the best way of supporting female-led business is through purchase of their products. In menswear and home goods, Bombinate protects and preserves the work of human hands by connecting craftsmanship brands to men seeking high-quality lifestyle products.

Knowledge and expertise. It is easier than ever to access specialized knowledge and expertise, from YouTube luxury watch videos to menswear forums and luxury handbag aficionados. Highsnobiety and Hodinkee are combined media and e-commerce destinations that provide not only information and expertise on modern aspiration and watches, respectively, but also product purchase opportunities.

Cultural moment/atmosphere. Right now, we are at the cultural moment of general life improvement. "Wellness" is a tab on almost any site, from fashion retail to selling plants. Products across industries get filtered through this mood, and are presented as the answer to the question of whether they make our lives better and more fulfilling, if they help us advance on the Maslow's hierarchy of needs, or whether they enrich us emotionally, mentally, and spiritually.

Story. Curation, by default, creates stories. Stories boost the relevance and significance of a product or a brand. They turn them into collectibles, lend them meaning and cultural purpose, and emphasize their social and communal dimension. LeBron James and Kim Jones tell their travel stories for Rimowa. In this way, they contextualize Rimowa luggage in a larger narrative of creativity and ambition.

Hobby and interest. Modern running and cycling brands are an example of the curation of an entire lifestyle around their customers' passion for the sport.

Trend and hype. For those wanting to know what's bestselling now, there's New York Magazine's The Strategist's or The Sill's most popular plants.

Location. A good cultural narrative cannot take place just anywhere. A provenance like South of France, Lower East Side on Manhattan, Harajuku in Tokyo, or Kreuzberg in Berlin are culture machines. Brands that emerged there capture more than a geographic location: they get the mood, the atmosphere, the time, and the community, along with a particular subculture and a taste. Streetwear brands like Supreme are unmistakably rooted in downtown New York; there is a strongly emphasized Parisian vibe of brands like Maje, Sandro, or Isabel Marant.

Personality or celebrity. The rise of social commerce goes straight into the heart of consumers buying curated product selections from each other, or as Steve Dool, head of Brand Partnerships at Depop, puts it: "There is something very 2020 about buying stuff from someone who made their name dancing or jumping off the side of a building or whatever." There's credibility in peer-to-peer curation, along with a shared taste: "another added benefit of allowing consumers to shop from people with similar interests and points of view, as opposed to brands that cater to their aesthetics or preferences," adds Dool. Elsewhere, modern art connoisseurs Justin and Hailey Bieber have been tapped by Paddle8 as curators.

Price. Popular iteration of curation by price is "gifts under $50." A lot of retail sites offer filtering by minimum and maximum price as well, but there's opportunity to make this filter more appealing by wrapping it up in a story of spending wisely or being smart.

Heritage, ritual, and tradition. The common perception is that a brand with a link to heritage and craft almost immediately achieves a veneer of rarity. This mechanism is often used in retrofit manner, with brands (and entire regions) clamoring to emphasize their provenance and heritage. Brand founders are often elevated to the level of artists. A modern brand that does this well is Aesop, which rooted its retail into its positioning as a "fabulist" and doubles down on the craft and tradition of storytelling in its brand behavior, through stores to brand magazine and content, to the website and events.

Bots as ultimate influencers

Third model of social influence is algorithmic personalization. In this iteration, brands will not hire existing influencers. They will create their own. To get a glimpse of this future, look no further than 15-second video app TikTok. Owned by Chinese AI-company ByteDance and known as Douyin in China, TikTok's core value proposition is algorithmic personalization.

Algorithmic personalization means that we get to enjoy highly appealing content regardless of who created it. We don't need to follow anybody or browse or search. Content is delivered to us based on an algorithmically created taste profile rather than socially. TikTok effectively wipes out social status as the influencer market's capital and taste as its currency. It creates the radically new kind of market where we equal our own taste profiles.

In this market, we are all potential influencers. On Douyin, many popular videos are not created by celebrities, but by ordinary people doing creative things in the form of life hacks or hashtag challenges, which serve as trending topics on the platform and regularly draw hundreds of thousands of people to participate in making videos on the same theme. In the West, we see this trend in the rise of dedicated enthusiasts turning their passions into how-to, leading to surge in popularity of topics like farming, house cleaning, cooking, and minding sheep. There are now more than 2.8 million posts tagged #farming on Instagram – and the same number of those tagged #cleaning. In China, Douyin also actively scouts for new talent in art and music schools and works with MCNs (multi-channel network) agencies specializing in turning "regular" people into Internet celebrities.

Second, in the influencer market of the future, bots wield the ultimate power of authenticity. Since the app is showing us only content that we already like, it teaches us which voices and perspectives are worth trusting. And because content that we like can come from literally anyone – an ordinary person as well as celebrity – it is perceived as more authentic than content created by an individual who was potentially paid for it. Authenticity is implied in the algorithm by design. Its content focus (versus influencer focus) is a powerful trust-building strategy.

The obvious danger here is that algorithms are not neutral. By default, they create filter bubbles and reflect the same biases as the humans who designed them. In case of widely used global apps like TikTok, any bias can quickly scale to potentially disastrous results. Content algorithms are also very far from being a "bicycle for the mind," as Steve Jobs put it. Instead, they are highly addictive, with potentially equally disastrous results for our brains and our social lives.

TikTok is a place of followers, each gifted with the opportunity to become a trusted and authentic leader. This opportunity is dictated by ebbs and flows of our likes. In the future of social influence, stars are not born. They are created by our collective taste and made popular via personalization algorithm.

All three social influence models have a strategic role to play in our marketing plans. We can benefit dramatically from understanding the opportunities, limitations, and costs and benefits of each. Ideally, we can make them work together and amplify each other. When we don't know what works, portfolio approach is our best bet.

Bibliography

Katz, Elihu and Lazarsfeld, Paul, *Personal Influence: The Part Played by People in the Flow of Mass Communications*, Free Press, 1955.

Watts, Duncan, *Social Change Relies More on the Easily Influenced than the Highly Influential*, University of Chicago Press Journals, 2007.

https://instagram-press.com/blog/2019/03/19/instagram-checkout/

https://www.wmagazine.com/story/hailey-bieber-justin-bieber-curate-paddle-8-auction/

https://variety.com/2018/biz/news/luka-sabbat-snap-spectacles-1203015434/

https://www.cosmopolitan.com/entertainment/celebs/a27623334/influencer-arii-36-shirts-2-million-followers/

https://lessonbucket.com/media-in-minutes/the-two-step-flow-theory/

https://www.cnn.com/2019/12/07/business/influencers-aldi-kroger-costco-publix/index.html

https://influencermarketinghub.com/influencer-marketing-2019-benchmark-report/

https://www.instagram.com/hidden.ny/?hl=en

https://shop.thehelm.co/

https://bombinate.com/

https://nymag.com/strategist/

https://www.thesill.com/

https://www.nme.com/blogs/the-movies-blog/netflix-fast-forward-viewing-opinion-2562569

https://books.google.com/books?id=4mmoZFtCpuoC

Why taste communities are the future of marketing

3

We are going through the imagined community renaissance, thanks to modern brands stepping in as the social constructs of belonging left vacant by traditional institutions of social cohesion, like organized religion, civil society institutions, and mass media. Consumer collectives are the new audience unit. In this chapter, I suggest that, instead of focusing on individuals, brand professionals should look at the communities these individuals belong to. When we shift our focus from an individual to their network of relationships, we start asking different questions: how the communities an individual belongs are structured, what is their dynamics, how the influence spreads within them, who are the most active and/or valuable members. This shift reveals not our inferred, but our actual, taste. Netflix's taste communities are a variation of this idea. Its 125 million global viewers are divided into 2,000 "taste clusters" that group people based on their movie and TV show preferences. Thanks to its banks of data, Netflix goes beyond the psychographics of its average customer. Applied to the world of physical objects, this approach transforms how trends, things, and ideas are created, bought, and sold. In this chapter, you will learn about what how consumer niches create and spread taste, how to target consumer collectives, and what are fan-made brands, created by imagined communities of fans that do not necessary know each other but share tastes, aesthetics, and interests.

"Nicole is careful with her spending, but under right circumstances is willing to splurge on herself if the mood strikes her," reads a typical consumer persona. Just like horoscopes, psychographic profiles are full of generic, unverifiable, ambiguous, and often contradictory language that supports a number of interpretations.

Personas also mask the inherent unpredictability of our tastes and the complex ways they interact. My sister-in-law lives in an affluent suburb of Chicago. She owns a piece of Away luggage (before its fall from grace) and gets newsletters from Everlane. On the surface, she is a HENRY (High Earning Not Rich Yet), but in reality, she is a middle-aged married mother of three who now has both brands because they relentlessly pursued her through direct mail discounts until she finally gave in.

Inferring about psychographics based on the products that people buy is unreliable. People buy the same things for wildly different reasons: there's a discount, they are in different moods at different times, other people have them.

Equally problematic is personas' focus on the individual, because it ignores the fact that people are social creatures. They belong to communities and are part of influence networks that they use to decide what to watch, read, buy, and pay attention to.

Thanks to the Internet and its numerous influence networks, products across categories are now more susceptible to trends than to individual preferences. A show becomes popular because a lot of people watch it, although it's entirely possible that a big chunk of the show's audience does it not because it reflects their interests or values but because everyone else they know is watching a show and they do not want to be left out (Netflix even unrolled the fast-forward viewing option for those).

Instead of focusing on individuals, we should focus on their relationships and look at the communities they belong to.

Netflix's taste communities are a variation of this idea. This streaming platform's 125 million global viewers are divided into 2,000 "taste clusters" that group people based on their movie and TV show preferences. At the same time, Netflix content is extensively tagged and based on these tags and their connections, divided into micro-genres. Micro-communities and micro-genres are then matched up.

Thanks to its banks of data, Netflix goes beyond the psychographics of its average customer. They know the relationship ("matchmaking") between its members and its content, and also useful things like how many hours of watched content per month makes its subscribers unlikely to cancel.

If we add the social dimension here and apply Netflix matchmaking to connect all sorts of products, services, and brands with networks of influence that consumers belong to, we get an approach that exceeds efficacy of personas. We get a dynamic portrait individuals, their sources of influence, and their most important relationships and activities. We can understand individuals better if we understand the complexity of their social network.

When we shift our focus from an individual to their network of relationships, we start asking different questions: how the communities an individual belongs are structured; what is their dynamics; how the influence spreads within them; who are the most active and/or valuable members? This shift reveals not our inferred, but our actual taste.

Counting how many people carry Away luggage at airport lounges and in which permutation with other brands tells marketers very little, aside of the fact that consumers are receptive to a persistent and repeated messaging, price deals, and social influence. It also dangerously focuses attention on the least valuable customer: the one that's price-sensitive and trend-susceptible and least likely to be brand-loyal.

Marketers can do better by focusing on one or more of these four scenarios:

Think about your brand in plural. Just as my Netflix isn't your Netflix, my pair of Off-White sneakers is not your pair of Off-White sneakers. It doesn't matter that Netflix is a platform and Off-White sneakers are a physical product: when we apply tagging system and shopping data, each product is worn in a manner that reflects its user.

Grow through the niches. Netflix brand isn't its shows. It's personalization. This positioning allows Netflix to create a global market made out of micro-communities with their niche tastes. In traditional economy, brands did the opposite. In order to scale, they had to appeal to as many people as possible, and cater to as mass, generic taste as possible. Now every brand can grow (and increasingly does) through taste clusters and niches, without reducing the product differentiation that attracts them all.

There are many doors in. Netflix personalizes more than movie recommendations – it also personalizes promo images of its movies and TV shows. Personalizing of not only what is recommended, but also how, can be applied to packaging, direct mail, newsletters, email communication, or paid social. The more diverse the creative execution, the wider the potential audience interested in different aspects of the product, service, or brand is – and more likely that someone will like it.

Target communities, not individuals. Every Netflix user belongs to three or four taste communities. Members of modern societies belong to many more. No two persons are exactly alike, even those that buy the same products, choose the same brands, and like the same content. There are those who enjoy foreign movies and travel documentaries, horror films and romantic comedies, Vineyard Vines and Everlane, sneakers and high jewelry. People are communities they belong to.

Rise of fan-made brands

Brands have yet to adjust their brand strategy to the fact that people are not only individuals, but that they also belong to communities and are members of a society. A good starting point is the idea of "imagined communities" (1983) coined by a political scientist Benedict Anderson. Anderson used the term to explain the sources of modern nationalism. An imagined community is bound together by a deep horizontal comradeship between people who haven't met and don't know each other, but have similar affinities, beliefs, interests, and attitudes.

Today, we are going through the imagined community renaissance. Modern brands stepped in as the social constructs of belonging, and as the links between culture and psychology left vacant by traditional institutions of social cohesion. Just as the newly roused national communities of the 18th and 19th centuries were ready to go to war in the name of their nation, today's modern brand fans are quick to cancel the opponents or go to war with the brand competitors.

Fan is short for fanatic, and some of the modern fans truly are. But, as a media scholar Henry Jenkins noted in *Textual Poachers* (1992), his ethnographic account of fandom, it is also a source of creativity and expression "for massive numbers of people who would otherwise be excluded from the commercial sector."

If Jenkins heralded participatory culture built by fans, modern brands herald participatory economy, where under the guise of fandom, fans do the (free) work for brands – or for each other. "More and more individuals are launching their own membership communities, aiming to bring people together around a shared interest," writes marketing strategist Dorie Clark in *Harvard Business Review* (2019). "Build your business one person at a time. Just focus on 100 people. If they love you, they will market the product for you and tell everyone else," said Brian Chesky, the founder of Airbnb. Today's brand fans give feedback on product designs, create content, wear and advocate brand products, and are featured in advertising materials. Nowhere is the psycho-cultural-economic dynamic of brand fandom more apparent than in streetwear, which, like any hobby — comic books, running, or underground music — requires a true devotion. Fervor for sneakers is simultaneously a source of one's social standing within their peer group and an investment asset (exactly how big is indicated by the size of the resale streetwear market in North America, projected to reach $6 billion by 2025).

Most successful brands today are fan-made, created by imagined communities of fans that do not necessary know each other but share tastes, aesthetics, and interests. Thanks to social media, everyone is (or can be) a tastemaker and content creator, endowed with a proverbial soapbox, as Glossier's founder Emily Weiss put it. An indeed, as the allure of influencers fades and brands start to recognize the growing influence that comes from ordinary people, creating a community has become a go-to brand-building strategy.

Tracksmith is a running apparel brand for amateur runners, aimed at celebrating the style, heritage, and culture of the sport. Rather than starting from social media and search ads, Tracksmith opted for growing slowly and steadily, often organizing races and events in its Boston store in order to forge a direct, human connection with its runners. High-end cycling brand Rapha created its cycling clubs to a similar end of community-creation and enforcing their mission of making the world a better place through cycling. Doen is a fashion brand of "thoughtfully designed clothing by women, for women," with a strong emphasis on community and its members. Outdoor Voices' fans think that movement is fun and love #doingthings, usually together. The Italian Vanity Fair's editor claims that she is not doing a magazine but building a network.

Brands with vibrant communities are perceived as more culturally credible than those without them, and more and more brands from fashion, beauty, sports, travel, media, and even CPG ask us to join their imagined communities. They figured out that using a direct contact with consumers to establish a strong base to build atop it is the surest way for a quick growth. And while a lot of them often do tap into an existing passion, hobby, or interest of their fanbase, like Patagonia, Tracksmith, or Harley Davidson, there are also those that are using it as a marketing shortcut. Emboldened by the success of its brand Off-White, the newly acquired holding company New Guards Group plans to conceive, produce, launch, and distribute modern streetwear brands.

> In the early 1990s, we were all rooted in some sort of subculture. For example, skateboarding, or graffiti, or punk rock. Versus brands today, they are not really rooted in any sort of subculture. They just sort of appeared out of nowhere.
>
> (Erik Brunetti, the designer behind the label FUCT in his interview with *The New York Times*)

In the famous members-only eating clubs of San Sebastian, Spain, everyone contributes, and the quality of the contribution (read: a cooked meal) defines one's social standing within a club – rather than their social and economic position in the outside world. Aligned with this cooking meritocracy is the post-signaling time among the modern affluent.

What micro-communities mean for aspiration

When disgraced Russian oligarchs make a hasty exit out of their country, they are often forced to leave their private planes behind. In a uniquely Russian entrepreneurial twist, these grounded Gulfstream G650 jets then became a coveted backdrop for Instagram photo sessions. The Moscow-based Private Jet Studio offers sanctioned jets rentals for two-hour photoshoots with a personal photographer for $191. Private Jet Studio's Instagram features women in lingerie casually hanging out at the plane entrance (as one does), dreamily staring through the window (looking at the tarmac), or casually reading newspapers. Some are even sleeping, which, given the two-hour rental limit, seems like a giant waste.

Renting a grounded private jet for the sole purpose of sharing images on Instagram is peak status affordance. It allows sharing the external codes of an aspirational lifestyle, minus the actual lifestyle itself. No matter, the main purpose is to accumulate a social following, likes, and to maintain an online persona, in hopes that this social capital can be monetized.

Veblen described how aspirants mimic affluence in their habits. Trends start among the upper class and then trickle down. The modern aspiration economy is not only about the reversal of this trend but also about its erasure.

Once aspiration moved into the domain of intangibles, it became invisible. How does one register "elevating the world's consciousness," which is collaborative workspace WeWork's mission statement? More from the WeWork files, Adam Neumann's wife allegedly requested for an employee to be fired because she didn't like their "energy." In the modern aspirants' world, where a person's "energy" is something to be invested in, nurtured, regularly checked upon, and evolved, this makes a perfect sense.

As aspiration, invisibility is different than dressing down or downright shabbily that has historically been exhibited by the British upper class. A lack of concern for one's clothes and appearance and for "what people think" is still social signaling, and conveys confidence in one's social standing and is expression of privilege of not caring.

The affluent today neither signal their status nor share on social networks their tangible and intangible capital. In its invisibility, and in its planned lack of social reach, modern status is like a self-quarantine.

If you think this is extreme, consider luxury bunkers and survival kits; in the age of emergency, which is increasingly becoming not an exception, but the norm, it's the richest that survive. A side note: if I were an investor, I would be all over luxury survival kits, remote destination evacuation routes, and survival hideouts.

"It is so good that I DON'T want to tell anyone about it," my Japanese facialist said about her new beauty routine. *Monocle*'s Tyler Brûlé recently wrote about NOT sharing the best of Tokyo nightlife with anyone but the *Monocle* team, and about recently taking a Zurich restaurateur and his wife on a secret private tour. Threat of the reverse network effects is real, and Mr. Brûlé has been avoiding it for years.

Japanese do secret and private well. There are more secluded, three-seat, no-photo bars than anywhere else. These places are small worlds: hard to get in, local, intimate, curated, and private. It's hard to see an economic rationale in having a three-seat bar, but volume and scale is not the business they are in. Unlike the Big Luxury's logic of producing more products to make more money, the business of the small and secluded is social distancing. Their value is in atmosphere, an experience, and a ritual. No wonder those who know about them protect their knowledge.

The other weekend I read a profile of a director of a major art show who talked, with pride, about her collection of snow globes: the tourist kind, not the high-end ones, although she can certainly afford them. Modern aspirants are Insta curators, Hodinkee community, Depop resellers, participants in menswear forums. Not always the richest, but the most plugged-in people around. They move in narrow, but influential circles where they get access and social standing, thanks to their knowledge, interest, cultural participation, or expertise. Their status in these small groups may be invisible to anyone outside – and that is the point. Their social influence happens in small worlds, and from there it trickles on to the wider culture.

The invisible and the small is rapidly spreading as a desirable, status-signaling social experience beyond Tyler Brûlé's world, Japanese bars, and menswear forums. Two things are driving it.

First, consumers increasingly assume that what they are seeing on social media is not real. Physical appearance can be altered and filtered, a lifestyle can be fabricated. A few years ago, Rapper Bow Wow posted a photo of himself apparently boarding a private jet. Shortly afterwards, another photo, taken at the same time of the alleged private flight, surfaced of Bow Wow on a commercial flight, typing on his phone. Influencers manipulate their appearances, timelines, and contexts.

Second, a carefully cultivated online persona is today the social norm. Having an uncultivated one is a way of conveying social distinction. Being one's "true self" – or its near approximation – is more aspirational than blending into the mass of aesthetically and materially similar online profiles. It's increasingly hard to tell the difference between, for example, Arielle Charnas, Chiara Ferragni, her mother, her sisters, and their countless look-alikes: the communication codes are all the same.

Many opt instead for a more real, meaningful, and uncultivated micro-network presence instead. In a micro-network, posing in a rented private jet becomes ridiculous, so different forms of social distinction take place, like closeness and belonging, knowledge and expertise, or talent and skill. Discreet and intimate social media groups are springing up everywhere, from finstas to selected WhatsApp groups, accompanied by the small-world apps (e.g. Kinship and Cocoon). Influencers also recognized the trend, and started charging premium for a more intimate follower interactions, via Close Friends and WeChat paywalls. Being oneself and freely sharing with a selected few seem to beat the effort of being a fake self with a mass. It's the social media iteration of private clubs, and again, the intimacy, the quality of experience, and the atmosphere are the draw.

Nowhere is this shift from mass model to value model more visible than in the modern restaurant scene. The National Restaurant Association claims that a 60 percent of restaurant meals are now consumed off-premises (2019). Ghost kitchens – establishments set up for the purpose of preparing food for delivery or pickup – are springing up in empty malls and parking lots and are shaping up into a big business. The trend of self-quarantine now spreads from Generation Z to millennials and the wider culture.

On the other end of the spectrum, there are supper clubs and home-cooking groups. Eating is neither their focus nor the most important purpose.

Supper clubs, which have in the past decade gained in popularity, are a uniquely American restaurant genre that dates back to the Prohibition in the 1920s. Little has changed in their format since then: a combination of dining, live music, and a social club, they are an all-evening entertainment destinations. Pop-up dinners are a more recent development, and a lot of them sprang around sharing one's culture, family history, and a local culinary tradition with an immediate micro-community of strangers.

Just like Japanese three-seat bars, supper clubs and pop-up dinners offer the ritual, the atmosphere, and the experience that UberEats cannot deliver. Once this scenario evolves further, the restaurant industry will split into two: the middle will disappear (the restaurants with ok food and ok setting, which is most of them right now), and those remaining in business will become very differentiated, very exclusive, or very expensive. They will offer either a food that doesn't travel well or an atmosphere and a ritual that can't be replicated. Some may even charge admission fee or have a cover charge. On the other end, there will be ghost kitchens, providing an infinite variety of food options and their fast and convenient delivery.

There are the three implications for brand strategy:

Strategic bifurcation, or splitting all the brands' product and service offerings into two. This strategy mimics what is already happening in a number of markets, where the middle is increasingly being hollowed out (fashion, apparel, travel, hospitality, media, furniture, food). On one end is the covetable experience, high-end product quality, and human-to-human interaction (Japanese three-seat bars model), and on the other is speed, convenience, scale, and a minimum viable product (ghost kitchens). Airlines and automotive industry are already doing this. In other categories, like CPG, this strategy is costly as it requires splitting a company's value chain into two. In a less costly iteration, high-end offering can exist in the form of a limited-time, periodic, value-added.

Strategy of controlled access. Modeled after supper clubs and pop-up kitchens, this strategy provides access to product, services, and experience bundles to a small number of customers. Keywords here are not only "access" but also "bundle," which – like pop-up dinner's focus on heritage and story of food – wraps the offering in a narrative. Tyler Brûlé's secret Tokyo is a version of this idea, where those close to the brand, willing to pay premium, or are trusted brand collaborators gain access. Another way is a version of "cover charge" where customers can select to pay (or earn) extra services, like speed of delivery, expanded product selection, or seat reservations in a restaurant. Examples are the food delivery monthly subscriptions, like Uber's Eats Pass, or paying fitness clubs extra to secure a preferred spot in a class.

Reviving the middle. A counterintuitive strategy is for a brand to strategically and purposefully focus on reintroducing the middle. This model has a strong social component: for example, in a bifurcated restaurant industry, we will lose gathering places for people from different backgrounds (this has been voiced in the critique of Sweetgreen's cashless policy, which has since been reversed). A lot of DTC brands, across categories, adopted "reviving the middle" strategy in the form of good-quality items at affordable prices and excellent service. The downside of this model is that it's costly, and most of these brands emulating it are VC-funded and not yet profitable. Scaling this model is also a challenge, as costs of supply, production, and distribution increase.

Bibliography

Anderson, Benedict, *Imagined Communities: Reflections on the Origin and Spread of Nationalism*, Verso, 1983.

Clark, Dorie, "How to Create an Online Community that People Will Pay for Harvard Business Review," September 25, 2019, https://hbr.org/2019/09/how-to-create-an-online-community-that-people-will-pay-for

Jenkins, Henry, *Textual Poachers: Television Fans & Participatory Culture*, Routledge, 1992.

https://en.wikipedia.org/wiki/Barnum_effect

https://sweettalkconversation.com/2016/06/02/the-rainbow-ruse/

https://www.businessinsider.com/what-is-a-henry-millennials-earning-six-figures-feel-broke-2019-11

https://review.chicagobooth.edu/economics/2019/article/demand-niche-products-growing

https://www.xxlmag.com/news/2017/05/twitter-roasts-bow-wow-private-jet/

https://medium.com/netflix-techblog/artwork-personalization-c589f074ad76

https://www.highsnobiety.com/p/cultural-credibility-brands/

https://www.cnn.com/2019/09/21/entertainment/cancel-culture-explainer-trnd/index.html

https://www.fastcompany.com/40523177/outdoor-voices-and-bandier-go-to-war-over-color-blocking-and-fans-are-picking-sides

https://www.mercurynews.com/2018/07/11/nicki-minaj-and-her-fans-go-on-the-attack-against-writer-who-pondered-a-mature-musical-direction-for-rapper/

williamwolff.org/wp-content/uploads/2015/01/jenkins-2992-conclusion.pdf

https://hbr.org/2019/09/how-to-create-an-online-community-that-people-will-pay-for

https://www.businessoffashion.com/articles/intelligence/stockx-to-become-first-billion-dollar-sneaker-reseller

https://www.nytimes.com/2019/05/21/style/streetwear-hypebeast-survey.html

https://www.businessoffashion.com/articles/news-analysis/vanity-fair-italia-editor-i-am-not-doing-a-magazine-i-am-building-a-network

https://www.saveur.com/inside-san-sebastians-members-only-eating-clubs/

Mimicry as taste
4

Why cultural sameness is
a matter of social design

The modern aspiration economy is filled with examples of products, services, and brands that are popular because they are sharable social symbols: MSCHF, Instagram Face, Baby Yoda, Rimowa luggage, matching pajama sets, minimalism, intermittent fasting, Peloton. Thanks to the Internet, products across categories are now more susceptible to trends than to individual preferences. It's easy to blame algorithms for the sameness of our taste choices, but the real culprit is us. Humans use social signals to quickly orient themselves in the world. On a daily basis, we actively classify one another by lifestyle, values, interests, and projected and perceived social standing. Based on taste displays, individuals make snap decisions – whether a person is like them or far away in taste space, and thus foreign. Just like crickets or light bulbs, albeit amplified with Instagram likes, Twitter hashtags, and other performance metrics, our taste signals get harmonized, so all of us end up looking the same, dressing the same, liking the same things, and visiting the same places. In addition to being a great mechanism in learning how to orient, belong, and present oneself in the world, imitation is responsible for social cohesion. In this chapter, you will find specific examples from the modern aspiration economy (coffee shops design, Airbnb aesthetics, Instagram "look") to analyze how social classification and social cohesion move culture toward the world that's harmonized and homogenous in taste.

Uptown or downtown. Billie Eilish or Justin Bieber. Zara or The Frankie Shop. Bagels or cronuts. Gucci or Louis Vuitton. Soulcycle or Tracy Anderson. Ibiza or Croatia. Rimowa or Muji. Vegetarian or not. Taste choices we make reflect where in society we belong, or aspire to belong. They are valuable social signals, and in the post-everything world, perhaps the ones that matter most.

There's been a lot of talk about the sameness of our taste choices – in music, fashion, interior design, entertainment, or physical looks. It's easy to blame algorithms for this, but the real culprit is us. We almost never make decisions independently of one another. Faced with abundance of choice, we rely on others to know what to buy, read, wear, or listen to. We also like the same things as others because we are social animals and want to share our experience with them.

There's also this. Similarly as our ancestors had to, as a matter of survival, quickly decide if a fellow Neanderthal was a friend or a foe, modern humans use social signals to quickly orient themselves in the world. On a daily basis, they actively classify one another by lifestyle, values, interests, and projected and perceived social standing. Based on taste displays, they make snap decisions whether a person is like them or far away in taste space, and thus foreign. Feeling cozy in our own taste space is largely responsible for the 37 *Avengers* movies and the *Top Gun* reboots to look forward to. Burning Man outfits, family pajama sets, Halloween costumes, weddings, craft breweries, and coffee shops all appeal to human tendency to revert to the recognizable and the familiar. Thanks to it, Spotify is now a music genre, one shorter and with memorable hooks in the first 30 seconds, in addition to being a streaming platform. TikTok is a music label. Amazon's clothing line does little more than to mimic what's currently popular.

TikTok, Netflix, or Spotify all use it to deliver content that we like, and that we are going to like more of. In this model, the platforms themselves – not brands or mass media or influencers – create popular trends, ideas, and aesthetics. Most popular songs on Spotify all bring their thunder in the first 30 seconds, because that's how long a song needs to be played for in order to count as a "listen." Instagram aesthetic shapes design of fashion items, retail stores, hotel lobbies, and product packaging. TikTok's "challenges," where people are prompted to recreate specific dances or routines, seeped into our culture, where brands react to each other's popular styles, and then reactions to reactions create trends (expect to see a lot more brands making Bottega Venetta's cloud bag or Jacquemus' Le Chiquito) and a lot more Hollywood franchises and sequels. Mimicry is elevated to the level of a trend.

In the past, it was easy to discern one's social standing by display of their economic power. But with both inconspicuous consumption and the rise of "installment economy," everyone can wear designer clothes and accessories, travel extensively, be an art collector, or have an interior decorator. Less affluent mimic behaviors, values, and tastes of the affluent; the affluent mimic sand crabs, rendering themselves all but invisible.

Faulty as they may be, snap judgments overpower decision-making. Processing complexity of any person, choice, or a situation is time-consuming and resource-draining. Snap judgments simplify the world. A very few people have the time or the mental bandwidth to sift through Forgotify.

Instead of learning about the world in every single situation, humans imitate what others are doing. Just like crickets or light bulbs, albeit amplified with Instagram likes, Twitter hashtags, and other performance metrics, our taste signals get harmonized, so all of us end up looking the same, dressing the same, liking the same things, and visiting the same places.

Nothing succeeds like success, the saying goes. With aggregate demand, success equals popularity: something becomes popular because a lot of people like it. Spotify, Amazon, TikTok, Instagram, all recommend what's already popular.

Regardless of how aggregate markets work, marketers love to assign every consumer choice with meaning and to provide infinite options to cater to consumer "uniqueness." They seem to forget that, more often than not, consumers do not eat kale because they watched a heartbreaking documentary about the meat industry. They eat it because, by doing so, they send social signals of being enlightened, wellness-obsessed, and socially conscious. They do not watch "Succession" because they like it; they watch it because their friends watch it and they want to participate in the shared experience.

In addition to being a great mechanism in learning how to orient, belong, and present oneself in the world, imitation is responsible for social cohesion. Social media platform TikTok is both a great metaphor and an actual example of this: its Challenges establish a sense of community, in the same way that streaming of the same music or entertainment creates a temporary bond among strangers.

Combined, social classification and social cohesion move culture toward the world that's harmonized and homogenous in taste (people need to know that they belong to the same community, and to know it quickly; they also need to know that their differences are not mortal.) Maybe in the USA today, we do need *Avengers* to feel like we still belong to the same nation. Algorithms are made by humans, and they replicate not only their biases but also their interpersonal and group behaviors responsible for holding societies together. If algorithms tend toward the outrageous, the flashy, and the comforting, that's because we do.

Both mechanisms, of social classification and social cohesion, also explain why, in the modern aspiration economy, brand affinity is created not economically, but socially – and why best loyalty programs treat their customers as community members.

From loyalty to membership

The irony of most of today's loyalty programs is that they aren't about loyalty at all. They have more to do with economic calculation and gain management than with the true affinity for a brand.

For example, there are programs that allow customers to earn points for following a brand or for writing a product review. This sort of bribery usually attracts the least loyal – and least valuable – audience who is mostly interested in the positive transaction utility and has a low brand investment (once they claim a reward, they can unfollow the brand). Within this calculative logic, installment payment plans like Afterpay, Affirm, and Klarna may be the biggest loyalty programs of all.

True loyalty is emotional and irrational, and often at odds with our survival instinct. To achieve it, brands are better off with membership programs than the point schemes. Figuring out a good membership scenario is even more important today with a proliferation of subscription models, private chat rooms, and an ever-increasing costs of paid social as the customer acquisition tool. Converting customers into subscribers and participating in consumer micro-networks are easier if they feel like members of a group.

Membership appeals to human irrationality. A lot of sneakerheads waiting in line all night to score a coveted item don't do it for resale; they do it for the badge value and the bragging rights. I had a hard time canceling my overpriced and underutilized fitness club membership because leaving a community is hard.

Membership is also a vehicle of the modern aspiration economy. It represents a shift from doing things for the benefit of others (conspicuous consumption), to a value model where we invest in things that benefit ourselves: access, knowledge, information, experience, privacy, belonging, self-actualization. In the modern aspiration economy, consumers are fans, influencers, hobbyists, environmentalists, and collectors. Membership programs are designed for them. Not as straightforward as loyalty programs, membership trades on social and cultural capital. Scoring an invite for the Château de Saran, the centerpiece of the Moët Chandon empire, doesn't have a price: "you cannot pay to come and stay at Saran, that is not the point. You have to be asked," says Stephane Baschiera, the president and CEO of Moët and Chandon in her 2019 interview with *The New York Times*. Members of the Prada's private club have been similarly selected by the brand. It's secrecy and insider knowledge that counts, because no one wants to deal with the dreaded reverse network effects. A martini at Alfred's wouldn't taste the same if everyone was invited. And indeed, best member clubs are surrounded by myth and mystery (The First Rule of Fight Club).

Go beyond traditional luxury, and this logic can be applied across categories. Any brand can create an invite-only club of people who are passionate about what the brand stands for (e.g. gender equality, sustainability, running, brand aesthetics) and aligned with what it seeks to do in the world. For example, there are buy-sell-trade communities thriving on Instagram and Facebook around specific fashion labels, including the private messaging groups for plus-size members to trade their items. YouTube hosts niche communities that sprang around watches, menswear, makeup, cleaning, farming, gaming. Individuals themselves are launching their own membership communities around their shared interest. Niche food, niche dinner clubs, and niche fashion magazines are proliferating, as do hyper-specialized gyms, intimate online spaces like group chats, and waiting in line for Glossier drops.

The keyword here is not necessarily prestige and exclusivity, but identity and belonging. There's a pure pleasure in the intimacy of consuming together, along with enjoying status within a community. Thanks to a membership in a community, a hypebeast gets access to new product drops and events. This is the domain of intangibles that most loyalty programs fail to deliver, and that membership excels in.

In recent years, even airlines, once the provenance of rigid, confusing, and unachievable miles programs, have evolved toward providing frequent, serendipitous, and rewarding products, experiences, and service that delight their customers. Once a provenance of collecting miles for a free banana in Economy Comfort, Delta seems to lead the way among the US Airlines. "The back row seat on a Delta flight gets you better service than a front row seat on American," wrote someone on Twitter, and "Packed flight, economy basic, middle seat, on lowest status tier and Delta still makes every touchpoint superb," was one of the comments.

Investing to make the each customer experience touchpoint rewarding in itself through small perks and attentive care is more motivating and creates greater brand affinity than just getting points. A pure behavioral economics is behind it: consumers prefer many small repeated gains and many incremental rewards instead of big infrequent ones. They'd rather find two $50 bills in two different places than a single $100 bill in one. Mental accounting is responsible for their perceptions of value, utility, cost, and benefits of something. If values and worth are basis of today's status, and if we spend more to accumulate social and cultural capital, bribing consumers with rewards for buying more products makes little sense.

Here is what works instead

Membership is micro

Indie bookstores, proliferation of private communication apps, "Close Friends" on Instagram Stories, and rise of neighborhood outposts of national chains are the opposite of a "bigger is better" model. It seems that we want to shop, entertain, and socialize in the same way we did at the turn of the last century, before mass media. "Build your business one person at a time. Just focus on 100 people. If they love you, they will market the product for you and tell everyone else," said Brian Chesky, the founder of Airbnb. Across categories, there has been a move toward smaller, more decentralized offerings revolving around personalization and hyper-focused inventory. Netflix is perhaps the most famous example with its global market made out of micro-communities with their niche tastes.

Membership is myth-making

Most coveted clubs have a myth and a tale surrounding them, by design. Cooking clubs of San Sebastian have a hefty dose of mystery surrounding them. Passerby can catch a glimpse of a gathering, a meal, a kitchen, or a group of people, without knowing what exactly it is all about. And that's exactly how the cooking clubs want it. One needs to earn membership, which is purely based on skill: status within a cooking club (and by proxy, in the wider community) is social and cultural, and not economic. A rich person and their driver are equally welcome, and if the driver turns out to be a better cook, they will enjoy a higher standing.

Membership is mentorship

Groups that activate a mentorship among their members offer a direct and clear value that makes the members stick and grows over time. Poshmark's Posh N Sip local events reward their sellers and keep them involved. Sellers have the opportunity to learn from others and share their experiences in, for example, inventory management, customer service, or photography tips. Fitbit similarly engages its members in coaching each other in exercise regimes. Glossier has a Slack channel where the brand superfans are the co-creators.

Membership is influence

Giving its members content and tools to create influence in their immediate and local groups lends social status and also organically and cost-
effectively expands the membership group. Lively's brand ambassadors
are given the opportunity and the tools to host their own Lively brand
events. Because social influence is inherently unpredictable and random
and everyone's a potential influencer, Uniqlo gave 100,000 customers free
samples of its heat tech apparel, hoping that some of them will catch on
and spread. On the other end of the spectrum, carrying a badge, a cultural
code of belonging to a private club, or invite-only community is the new
social capital. Having a limited-edition product, carrying a Colette tote
or a copy of a *Courier Magazine*, wearing a Comrades race T-shirt are all
signals of influence.

Membership is identity

Brands reflect their position in culture through their members. Fans of
Rothy's, a sustainable shoe brand, spontaneously gathered around identifi-
cation with a shared lifestyle. Part social club, and part marketplace, these
groups swap, resale, and share everything, from shoes to friends to life
moments to recommendations. Ethel's Club is a private membership club
designed for people of color, which aims to shift the narrative around social
clubs. Tracksmith caters to its customers' identity as runners and rewards
it via social capital. Its $100 store credit bonus is designed for runners who
break their own personal record while wearing Tracksmith. "Gucci Open
House" is an eight month-long series that takes fans into the homes and
lives of selected Gucci diehards.

Brands faced with lackluster results of their loyalty programs should consider the following benefits of switching to a membership scenario:
Membership recognizes that a brand's consumers are not a monolithic
group, but a network of subgroups and niches. A good membership
program's unique value proposition, messaging, benefits, and how they
are conveyed through look, feel, and tone of voice are tailored to each
of these subgroups and niches. There should never be one membership
program; there should be many, for each of the consumer groups. The
likelihood of each consumer benefiting from personalized communication and benefits is higher than them benefiting from a one-size-fits-all
points scheme.

Membership can do a lot of a marketing campaign's heavy lifting. Consumers have intense affinity toward brands that clearly and consistently put forward their purpose, codified through specific brand behaviors, like physical retail, events, content, community initiatives, or partnerships. Offering a direct access to this purpose, be it sustainability, or female empowerment, or corporate responsibility, organically creates a sense of membership in a community of others who support the same purpose.

Membership activates learning. The first step here is to define the lifestyle area that members can refine, improve upon, and be more informed about. Depending on a brand, this can be sports (how to be a better athlete), fashion (sustainability, supporting female founders), grocery (cooking, nutrition), wellness (self-care rituals), beauty (organic ingredients, regiments), CPG (ingredients, carbon footprint, fair trade). This lifestyle area needs to stem from a brand's role in culture, environment, or society.

Membership recognizes and rewards a brand's superfans. It amplifies their social and cultural capital through content, tools, access, products, events, and their physical and digital properties.

Membership is the answer to the "why are we coming together?" question. It emphasizes the passion, interests, values, and identity that already bind a brand's audience together. Micro-social media apps like Discord to HeyKinship to Cocoon to YouTube and Instagram niches help: membership starts small, stays focused, and earns trust. A membership program can further own a hashtag for products resale, like #JamieandTheJonesForSale did, or can create a commercial symbol that encourages a common sentiment, like Colette or Tiffany did.

Compared to these membership opportunities, points-based systems come across as lazy. In the modern aspiration economy, brand affinity is created not economically, but socially. In the old school model, membership offered modest, slow, and infrequent monetary gains. In the modern aspiration economy model, consumers use their membership to advance their social, cultural, and environmental capital. They also use it to develop and refine their taste.

Nice things for good life

Nice Things is a monthly magazine that features items like Hina dolls and rice bowls, photographed against a clean, monochromatic backdrop. There are also images of people cooking, foraging, farming. Everything is simple, artisanal, understated, wholesome. It promotes "good life with nice things."

There are more periodicals like this. Ordinary is a fine art photography quarterly focused exclusively on creative riffs on a single everyday object (cabinets, a mop, a sink). &Premium is a "guide to a better life." It is dedicated to artisanal coffee roasters, hand-crafted knives, flower bouquets, and ceramic bowls. There are entire pages on a "nice scent," "spring bouquet," "beautiful shoes."

What links them is their focus on the ordinary. "The ability to see great beauty in the everyday objects around you is a rare and precious gift." For this, thank (or blame) our post-growth age. Climate emergency; global pandemic; aging population; and the new cultural, social, and environmental capital create new sources of value.

In the past, more was always more. Brands promised that we would be more attractive, more accomplished, more affluent, only if we bought more of their products. "Buy more, save more" was marketers' favorite call to action. Similarly, bigger was always better: a bigger house, a bigger car, a bigger sofa, a bigger logo.

Today, more important than a Mari Kondo lifestyle is a general shift to micro in our relationship with the world. There's micro-socializing, micro-attention, micro-experiences, micro-focus, micro-expectations. Unable to succeed economically, millennials are turning their attention to everyday things with an almost obsessive, laser-like focus. Can't afford a home? Get a great mattress. Cook with nice cutlery. Don't have a retirement account? Enjoy looking at your sill filled with plants. Invest in a beautiful spatula.

Modern brands turned millennial existential anxiety into a taste regime

A taste regime shapes how consumers use objects in everyday life. "We want not just to be a provider of Japanese coffee equipment, but to focus on the education of the Japanese way of home brew, the Japanese coffee culture, and the art of coffee itself," says the founder of Kurasu, a specialty coffee and artisanal brewing equipment site.

Originally coined by authors Zeynep Arsel and Jonathan Bean (2012), a taste regime defines how consumers create routines and meaning around objects. A taste regime turns a particular taste into practice through different consumption patterns, leisure activities, vocabulary, and ways of socializing. For example, a taste regime around Peloton defines how and when and why a person uses their bike, what they wear while riding it, how they interact with it, and how they talk to others about it. A taste regime around Great Jones kitchenware articulates the specifics of how and when to use it, what other cookware or dinnerware to use it with, what to cook with it, and the exchanges with the community that's created around it.

Kurasu pairs its subscription coffees with stories and photos of the people behind the beans. Every time brands includes photos of artisans in their packaging, have a carefully curated Instagram account that conveys a particular aesthetic, or put their social mission at the front-and-center of their messaging, they contextualize their products in a taste regime. Haus' homepage features attractive photography of attractive people drinking aperitif and having fun.

Through taste regimes, modern brands introduce new meanings in our everyday activities: cooking, socializing, bathing, decorating, dressing, caring for pets or plants. "Power and pleasure of making food with your own hands" replaces cooking. "Minimizing environmental impact" replaces buying a dress. "Boosting our creativity" replaces buying plants. Through meaning and values, a taste regime makes our interactions with everyday objects more intentional. It transforms our home and our daily routines, and it cultivates our taste and refines our sensibilities.

It also renews our relationship with everyday products by making it more creative: having nice kitchenware inspires us to cook more elaborate meals. Having a artisanal coffee equipment and speciality coffee shipped to us from across the world inspires us to create a coffee-drinking daily ritual. Thanks to taste regimes, we get more joy out of the everyday. We also adopt a new mechanism for social distinction and status signaling. A taste regime provides social links and holds a taste community together, and sets apart one taste community from another. Lululemon's taste regime is vastly different than Monocle's, which, in turn, is vastly different than GOOP's.

In addition to pushing their taste regimes forward, modern brands actively aestheticize our everyday life. Products we buy, our faces and bodies, our experiences and leisure, our living spaces and bookshelves are all increasingly transformed into works of art. "Everyday life is an art, as art is part of everyday life" is the modern branding's mantra, fed by the massive offering of Instagram inspiration.

The current construction of life as a visible work of art has been decades in the making. It is an outcome of simultaneous deinstitutionalization and commercialization of art that took place when the pop art of Andy Warhol, Roy Lichtenstein, and Robert Indiana made its way into museums. The fine art simultaneously spread into fashion, design, pop culture, and architecture. Back in the 1980s, New York City designer Willi Smith invited artists, architects, performers and graphic designers to join his project of making art part of daily life. Today, Virgil Abloh transforms mundane objects (T-shirts, boots, rugs) into works of art through quotation marks. Fashion stores are displaying art, and museums are selling merch. Moschino's Spring Summer 2020 collection took inspiration from Picasso. Undercover worked with Cindy Sherman on a collection. Zadig & Voltaire shop in New York City's Soho neighborhood features a stone sculpture with the "do not touch" sign.

In its 2020 iteration, pervasive investment in the aesthetics means constant internal and external self-perfecting (in my Tribeca fitness studio, I often see women at various stages of this process). Makeover shows like *Bridalplasty*, *Million Dollar Decorators*, or *100% Hotter*, tell consumers how to redesign their face, their house, and their life. Nothing is ever redesigned at random, so the makeover shows emphasize a sense of purpose: an aesthetically worthy life is not lived spontaneously, but stylistically. (An outcome is that a total lifestyle image put forward is often more impressive than a person behind it.)

GOOP is the prime example of aesthetically worthy living. GOOP fans are prompted to be continuously attuned to appearance, as even the smallest and the most mundane details of the everyday can be reworked into a sensorially and stylistically pleasing experiences that come with intention (self-care, self-actualization, a more loving home, the more fulfilling relationships).

Today, aesthetic innovation gives competitive edge. Innovativeness is not in having superior product properties or novel tech, but in the emphasis on aesthetics and experience (consider how GOOP-endorsed products have been accused of deceptive health claims yet continue to be popular). Successful brands ingrain themselves in the cultural context, not a market segment. Off-White, Kanye, Glossier, White Claw, Haus, GOOP all introduce new meaning in society and culture by linking social trends with their products. They create cult objects – Balm Dotcom, Jade Egg, Tesla, Jordan 1 x Off White – that serve as totems in their taste communities. (Peloton advertising regularly depicts their bikes as cult objects in shrine-like settings.) Modern brands are innovative because they combine the aesthetic experience, identity building, and social display.

There are three implications for brand strategy:

Create collections (rather than product ranges). A collection gives identity to everyday products. In the crowded industrial goods landscape, an identity is the key product differentiator: packaging, naming, color palette, signature design details, and product shapes, like the chick-shaped hand sanitizer in pastel colors by Olika, make products stand for something more than their function and differentiates them from commodities. A collection enforces product identity, ensures its continuity, and connects products into a narrative.

Trade in exchange value, not in use value. Use value is defined by a product's functionality. Exchange value is defined by a product's social appeal. These days, a competitive advantage is not in how it works, but in how it looks. A usable product or a functional tech is almost a given. It's the aesthetic and stylistic properties of products that matter. A social hit becomes a market hit. Focus your competitive strategy on how to insert your products in the socio-cultural exchange system, like White Claw did, not on their market position based on performance and price.

Invest in the aesthetic innovation. Infuse taste and meaning into ordinary consumption. Think how your products and services not only fulfill their basic functions but also add an aesthetic and social dimension to their attributes and turn them into social links that hold together taste communities. Fenty Beauty's "Beauty for all" call to action is a good example. Rihanna enriched her product innovation (over 50 shared of foundation) with a strong female entrepreneurship angle and narrative. Rihanna is a bold, outspoken, and independently-minded female founder, and we wholeheartedly root for her to succeed. Together with editorial content, retail environments, messaging, images and symbols, and social engagement, product aesthetics creates taste regimes that shape our everyday life. Creating a taste regime takes time, practice, an ongoing social engagement, and images and symbols – and distinguishes brands that endure from those that don't.

Bibliography

Zeynep, Arsel and Bean, Jonathan, "Taste Regimes and Market-Mediated Practice," *Journal of Consumer Research* 39(5): 899–917, 2012.

https://mommematch.com/familymatchingeverything/

https://www.youtube.com/watch?v=OP6JGlv32nw

https://www.margaretwheatley.com/articles/irresistiblefuture.html

https://www.ranker.com/list/uncanny-mimics-in-nature/anna-lindwasser

forgotify.com/

https://www.nytimes.com/2020/01/20/style/prada-private-club-paris-couture-week.html

https://www.nytimes.com/2019/05/23/style/moet-chateau.html

https://twitter.com/HansDeLeenheer/status/1218151790883098626?s=20

https://twitter.com/tomfgoodwin/status/1220019850216538113?s=20

https://www.uniqlo.com/us/en/featured/heattech-giveaway

https://www.instagram.com/nicethingsmagazine/?hl=en

https://academic.oup.com/jcr/article-abstract/39/5/899/1795003

https://uproxx.com/life/white-claw-flavors-ranked/

https://www.thecut.com/2019/11/instagram-kevin-systrom.html

https://thebaffler.com/latest/luxury-on-the-installment-plan-del-valle

https://www.modernretail.co/platforms/how-poshmark-uses-small-local-events-to-drive-engagement-and-retention/

https://www.wearlively.com/pages/join-the-lively-crew

https://www.instagram.com/explore/tags/jamieandthejonesforsale/

https://www.businessoffashion.com/articles/professional/from-tiffany-blue-to-louboutin-red-the-power-of-owning-a-colour

ordinary-magazine.com/

https://www.instagram.com/and_premium/

https://www.newyorker.com/magazine/2020/02/10/can-we-have-prosperity-without-growth

https://kurasu.kyoto/

https://www.lyst.com/shoes/off-white-co-virgil-abloh-for-walking-cowboy-boots-7/?product=JEKHVSK&link_id=636929433&_country=US&size=38&show_express_checkout=true&atc_medium=cpc&atc_content=USA-PLA-Off-White+c%2Fo+Virgil+Abloh+Boots-Clothing+%26+Accessories+%3E+Shoes+%3E+Boots-CSS+Vacherin-no&atc_country=USA&atc_source=google&atc_grouping=Google-PLA-EXPRESS&atc_campaign=USA-PLA-EXPRESS&atc_type=pla&sem_id=A2427224057&gclid=Cj0KCQjwpLfzBRCRARIsAHuj6qXIPhyVmS2IqIGpTtd18u4eCEqB9cz4Tea2Ssw4Z4_J85oxT7zPL8AaAi_REALw_wcB

https://stockx.com/off-white-ikea-keep-off-rug-200x300-grey-white?country=US&currencyCode=USD&utm_source=google&utm_medium=cpc&utm_campaign=OD-Segment-Collectibles-New_Desktop(US)&utm_campaignid=6664381435&content=387012599923&keyword=&gclid=Cj0KCQjwpLfzBRCRARIsAHuj6qVRDwN_7iEYEnnWJDFSmbBV8-59Cj63-xi_HXU9Iy71u7Re7gzrWBoaAvpeEALw_wcB

https://www.standard.co.uk/fashion/moschino-mfw-ss20-a4242186.html

https://www.nbc.com/bridalplasty

https://www.bravotv.com/million-dollar-decorators

https://www.netflix.com/title/80234414

https://arstechnica.com/science/2020/02/goop-violating-court-order-with-yet-more-bogus-health-claims-watchdog-says/

https://www.businessinsider.com/people-on-twitter-are-ripping-apart-pelotons-unrealistic-ad-campaigns-2019-8

https://www.pjstudio.ru/

https://www.instagram.com/privatejetstudio/?hl=en

https://www.demilked.com/magazine/wp-content/uploads/2017/10/instagram-photoshoot-grounded-private-jet-studio-moscow-13.jpg

https://collegecandy.com/wp-content/uploads/sites/5/2017/11/private-jet.jpg?resize=750,425

https://images.ladbible.com/thumbnail?type=webp&url=http://20.theladbiblegroup.com/s3/content/fa0369b259ea1879599d3104e59beb49.png&quality=70&width=648

https://hbr.org/2020/02/the-mystery-of-the-2000-ikea-shopping-bag

https://www.ft.com/content/7938752a-52a7-11ea-90ad-25e377c0ee1f

https://www.nytimes.com/2019/07/23/style/boris-johnson-and-the-rise-of-silly-style.html

https://www.nytimes.com/2019/08/13/us/apocalypse-doomsday-capitalists.html

https://www.vox.com/the-goods/2020/3/2/21151040/disaster-prep-survival-prepper-kit-judy-kim-kardashian-hurricane-fire

https://www.nytimes.com/2020/03/05/style/the-rich-are-preparing-for-coronavirus-differently.html

https://www.instagram.com/mist_beauty/

https://www.ft.com/content/71a90a26-0fcb-11e7-a88c-50ba212dce4d

https://en.wikipedia.org/wiki/Small-world_network

https://www.instagram.com/p/B9SPkhOnTeY/

https://www.independent.co.uk/arts-entertainment/music/news/bow-wow-private-jet-instagram-fake-stock-photo-commercial-flight-pictures-a7727996.html

https://www.instagram.com/ariellecharnas/?hl=en

https://www.instagram.com/chiaraferragni/?hl=en

https://www.instagram.com/marinadiguardo/?hl=en

https://www.instagram.com/valentinaferragni/

www.heykinship.com

https://cocoon.com/

https://www.voguebusiness.com/companies/influencer-paywall-what-it-means-for-fashion-brands

https://www.restaurant.org/Downloads/PDFs/Research/research_offpremises_201910

https://qz.com/quartzy/1748191/how-millennials-became-a-generation-of-homebodies/

https://thebaffler.com/downstream/streambait-pop-pelly

https://www.theverge.com/2016/8/3/12325104/airbnb-aesthetic-global-minimalism-startup-gentrification

https://www.newyorker.com/culture/decade-in-review/the-age-of-instagram-face

https://www.olikalife.com/

The 4Cs

5

Brand strategy meets the modern aspiration economy

At the time of Veblen, brand strategy was simple: marketers aimed their communication at targets defined by their household income and purchasing habits and their messages encouraged consumption of commodities as a way to accrue status. Now they have the opportunity to flip the script by focusing on one or more of the 4Cs: content, community, collaborations, and curation. In this chapter, you will find success stories from each of the four pillars and explain why and how they modernize culture, society, and businesses.

At some point during our trip to Japan in February 2020, I stopped by the new Louis Vuitton flagship in Osaka. Much talk has been made of LVMH's recent foray into hospitality, and of the Louis Vuitton's first-ever cafe and a restaurant in particular. I was intrigued.

The building is surely distinctive enough. It has a facade made out to look like the sails of a the traditional Japanese Higaki-Kaisen cargo ship, a nod to Osaka's naval history. But take the elevator to the 7th floor to Le Café V, and you'll find yourself in much less impressive setting. The space is stuffy. There are conflicting aesthetics and a very 1980s vibe (and not in a good way). The terrace has no view, but a lot of Tiffany blue chairs. I completely missed the artwork by Tracey Emin despite (or maybe because) it was placed right in front of the elevator. The crowd was mostly clad in LV garb and wasn't particularly sophisticated. Tourists mingled with provincial businessmen. Most people seemed to be there so they can take an Insta (myself included).

All of this seems to be exactly the purpose of this establishment, and of many more to come per LVMH's ambitions. One doesn't go to a Louis Vuitton restaurant for the food or cocktails; they go there to show and tell.

It's great to claim that this is all in the name of the brand projecting a lifestyle, but let's call spade a spade: taking a photo in LV cafe signals status in the same way that a LV bag does. Louis Vuitton having a restaurant just confirms what LV already is a traditional status-signaling, high-end fashion brand. It's not a reflection of one's lifestyle, but of their social affordance.

In the modern aspiration economy, social affordance is accrued in the same way that material goods are, but in the social domain: a significant social following, a carefully curated online persona, a witty social copy, meticulously composed Instagrams, or as many Insta stories from global locations/events/experiences as possible.

Both lifestyle and social affordances reflect a shift in spending patterns from tangible goods to intangible service and experiences, and this makes it easy to confuse them. Modern brand strategy is to blame: in the flattened modern aspiration landscape, where retail, hospitality, media and entertainment, experiences, and service are all mixed together, proclaiming a company to be a standard-bearer of a lifestyle is seen both as a competitive advantage and a wider reason for its being.

Categories from cooking to drinks to activewear to grooming to interior design, all offer great social affordances in the modern aspiration economy, but few manage to reach the level of a lifestyle.

In contrast, take Muji, which, over the past four decades, grew into a brand that reflects and supports the global consumer lifestyle. I experienced it first-hand when I visited Muji's new store-plus-hotel in Ginza. The hotel is a seamless part of Muji's retail establishment and is easily accessed via escalators that connect all of the floors. It's a minimalistic, low-key setting with a lounge, a bar, and a lobby, all in warm walnut tones. The vibe was welcoming, functional, and meticulous, just like a brand itself. There were some guests checking in, but no one cared to take a photo (except myself) or lingered just to be able to tell they were there. One can say that this is because Muji isn't a status marker of LV's magnitude, and that's exactly the point: it is a lifestyle brand, not a social affordance.

Having a catchy mission statement, sans serif font, Instagrammable packaging, a retail "experience," a photo aesthetic, or <insert here> doesn't turn a brand into a lifestyle. It is a PR trick that hardly makes a brand at all.

Rise and fall of GMO brands

Like GMO food, GMO brands[1] are the overgrown, monstrous, and tasteless versions of the real thing. They show up out of nowhere, grow rapidly, thanks to the steroid VC money, and reach outsized proportions before imploding or rotting. There are a lot of GMO brands: Nasty Gal, Groupon, Away, Everlane, Brandless, Outdoor Voices, Greats, Honest Company, Modcloth, Harrys, Peloton, Blue Apron, Bonobos, WeWork.

As quickly as they mushroom, GMO brands can implode. A few months ago, cultural publication The Verge exposed internal culture at the millennial-beloved luggage brand Away. "Bullying," "cutthroat," and "clique-y" were just some of the terms that former employees used to describe it. At the same time, venture capitalists rallied around the brand, dismissing the accusations. As one VC put it: "to build a $1B+ disruptive business requires speed and intensity. Startups are hard, period."

Rather than a heartfelt defense of visionary entrepreneurs chasing their dreams and breaking a few things in the process, this sentence reveals the deeply faulty foundations of VC investing today.

It has long been known that the short time horizon of the VC model stifles true innovation. While a new luggage or CBD brand can (and regularly does, per The Verge's article) speed up their growth to meet exits, startups working with AI, blockchain, or biotechnology require longer implementation horizons. They are unlikely to have a breakthrough within the timelines enforced by VCs. Couple this with a decrease in federal funding of science over the last 40 years, and it's clear that we need a new model of investment.

VCs rarely seem to think about how ideas they fund fit within the existing social and economic infrastructures. Beyond reckoning with the pace of scientific innovations, the VC industry needs a reality check: as Uber, Tesla, Deciem, WeWork, and now Away, Outdoor Voices, and Everlane show, VC-fueled startups are not helped to the same business and operational standards as their publicly traded counterparts.

The fact that it's never been easier and cheaper to start and grow a venture should force us to be disciplined about addressing their negative externalities. VCs rarely seem to think about how ideas they fund fit within the existing social and economic infrastructures. "There is nothing innovating about underpaying someone for their labor and basing an entire business model on misclassifying workers," California State Senator Maria Durazo said of Uber. Benefits of Amazon's two-day (and soon to be one-day) shipping were welcome until they started clogging our streets and our landfills and killing passers-by. Airbnb and Instagram turned cities and neighborhoods into consumable, picture-perfect destinations.

Companies ignore problems like treating employees unfairly and failing to build a nurturing work culture. Those problems don't get fixed as the companies scale.

VC industry seems unwilling to acknowledge network externalities that don't benefit it. It also seems unwilling to admit that it's destroying economic value by rewarding growth metrics versus profitability metrics. The result is a breakneck push for growth at all costs, which can make companies ignore problems like treating employees unfairly and failing to build a nurturing work culture. And indeed, during the coronavirus pandemic, companies that have been called out for their poor internal cultures and questionable employee treatment, like Everlane, Away, and The Wing, were those that were first to fire and furloughed their staff in order to keep themselves on the growth track.

These "original sins" don't get fixed as the companies scale. Lavishly funded by venture capital, startup brands are in the position to undercut incumbents on price and service, all the while being unprofitable. The result is that money-losing companies can go on undercutting competition far longer than before.

But then come the IPOs. They expose that a lot of the much-hyped startups are less viable than they seem. In its growth period, Casper was losing $157 on each mattress, due to $305 in marketing spend on each sale. This unsustainable marketing spend was a desperate measure: there are currently over 175 other direct-to-consumer mattress brands to choose from, reports CNBC. The same story repeats across categories: cookware, plants, athleisure, footwear, accessories, skincare, wellness, homeware, protein drinks, shaving products, and so forth. A much crowded DTC space makes it harder for a brand to stand out. Compared to legacy brands, DTC aesthetic and distribution was novel and an easy competitive advantage. But once DTCs started competing with each other, they realized that their look and distribution is table stakes. Their competitive differentiation disappeared overnight.

In February 2020, Casper's IPO valued the company about $600,000 lower than its last private fundraising round. In the same month, Brandless, unable to meet its financial targets, stopped operations and laid off 90 percent of its employees, reports Protocol. Also in February of 2020, Outdoor Voices' co-founder and CEO, Tyler Haney, was forced to resign due to a reported $2 million monthly losses on $40 million of annual sales, reported Buzzfeed.

According to GlobalData, VC funding for early-stage startups declined in January 2020. Stories of DTC bubble started circulating in late 2019 and early 2020. Mary Meeker, in her 2019 Internet Trends Report, similarly noted that DTCs have a hard time with customer retention and less aggressive, but more sustainable audience growth. Simply, a lot of companies raised quickly a lot of money, without a clear path to profitability and exit plans. The pressure for quick growth is real, and it is taking a real toll on internal company cultures and treatment of employees. "We prioritized business growth over cultural growth," said Audrey Gelman, one of the founders of women's co-working space The Wing, in her February 2020 Fast Company confessional.

All VC-fueled startup brands follow the same software-inspired Silicon Valley playbook of the Rapid Brand Building. An obvious oxymoron, Rapid Brand Building happens when a company funnels its VC funds into brand aesthetics and the tone of voice, relentlessly repeated through witty PR blasts and equally relentlessly supported by the mainstream business press.

This is not enough

Tone of voice is not a brand

Being chatty, witty, and approachable only masks the missing cultural link that ensures brand durability. It also masks the missing unique value proposition. GMO brands do not compete on the actual business value, like technical innovation, design, or product quality. Away's sells Muji knockoffs. Casper's subway riddles didn't do anything to fend off its lackluster IPO. Competing on a tone of voice is not a real and durable advantage.

Having a lot of followers is not a cultural voice

A cultural voice is someone who's earned their stripes and not just tells a tale.

> In the early 1990s, we were all rooted in some sort of subculture. For example, skateboarding or graffiti or punk rock. Versus brands today, they are not rooted in any sort of subculture. They just sort of appeared out of nowhere.
>
> (notes Erik Brunetti, the designer behind the label FUCT)

Designers like flea markets not only because they are aware of circularity of fashion trends, but also because they can riff of known cultural references. A cultural voice is achieved through dialogue and an exchange with other cultural forms: Balenciaga and Hello Kitty, Valentino and Henry Rousseau, Sacai and Funkadelic, Stella McCartney and Dick Straker, Dries Van Noten and Christian Lacroix.

PR doesn't build brands

PR agencies are not in the business of brand building, no matter how much they'd like to or claim to be. They may optimize the brand for "cultural moments" and do the modern version of propaganda (repeat, repeat, repeat), but they do not have the strategic and creative know-how needed for building legendary brands. Nike's chilling tribute to Kobe Bryant was done by a creative powerhouse, not a PR company. To avoid becoming GMO, emerging brands should take notice and invest in working with the brand building pros.

A well-executed media blitz is not a creative campaign. Having a perfectly planned rollout creates momentary awareness, but rarely makes lasting brand associations. In contrast, great creative stays with us for decades: vintage Coca-Cola ads, anytime LEGO ads, Apple ads from the 1980s (Think Different, 1984). Great creative's lasting appeal is in its craft, and sometimes even art – and because it provides infinite number of memes, references, clues, and myths that then assume the social life of their own. Creative's job is to make the raw material from which consumers compose and socialize the brand image, and, together with other elements of marketing communication, experiences, partnerships, and events, to create a recognizable universe of cultural associations, values, and experiences.

Delayed gratification is a feature, not a bug

Performance marketing and paid social carpet-bombing, no matter how targeted, do not create a human connection that all durable brands have and that makes them durable in the first place. A quick rush of sales following a paid social campaign or a stunt should not be a sign of positive ROI, but an inverse measure of brand loyalty. A human connection doesn't mean having just a group of superfans (after all, Outdoor Voices excelled there), but reaching a large number of taste communities and consumer networks. Allowing time for organic brand discovery is critical in this process: different consumer groups need it randomly, and they serendipitously discover a brand through their own networks. Rimowa, for example, didn't become an affluent status symbol of the millennials overnight. It took a lot of small steps, over months and years, to create positive brand associations and change the brand perception from a stodgy German luggage maker (albeit the one with high-quality products with strong reputation) to the hottest modern status symbol.

Brands require devotion

It's easy to forget that Supreme has been around for 25 years. Like comics or underground music, a streetwear habit in the 1990s required dedication. There used to be holy sites, like Canal Street Jeans, Phat Farm, or Triple Five

Soul. Today, there are myths, associations, and other sneakers or T-shirts that preexist the current releases and drops. Supreme has a narrative that exploits and highlights a relationship to the past: the references, the history, and the story. Thanks to it, Supreme today can successfully brand a brick and sell a punching bag on Grailed for $1475.

Trust requires time

With his idea of pre-contractual solidarity, founder of sociology Émile Durkheim proposed that there needs to be some general conditions of exchange before and outside of any specific interaction. Hermès orange, Louboutin red, and Tiffany blue quickly signal a shared understanding of the "general conditions of exchange" and create trust between a consumer and a brand. So does a brand mission. LEGO's mission is to "inspire and develop the builders of tomorrow." In contrast, Lululemon wants to "elevate the world by unleashing the full potential within every one of us," which is, perhaps fittingly for this brand, a yogababble (Galloway, 2019).

Just as GMO food doesn't do anything nutritionally for humans, GMO brands don't do anything for culture or for their company's long-term business success. Without a connection to culture, Coca-Cola is just a carbonated water and syrup. Today's VC time horizons do not allow for the next generation of Coke legends; instead, they churn Coke Lifes.

This is what works instead.

The 4Cs

Helena Glazer is a fashion and beauty influencer who goes under Instagram handle brooklynblonde1. On March 30, she posted a photo of herself in the head-to-toe Everlane look, a mere couple of days after Everlane fired all of its union workers and was publicly called out for it by Bernie Sanders.

Both in her website post and in her Instagram comments, she was called out for supporting a brand with the obviously unethical practices. "Maybe reconsider supporting Everlane. They are under heat and controversy for laying off their workers for wanting to unionize, which says a lot about Everlane," one Instagram comment read. "It's hard for me to even consider buying anything from Everlane having in mind their latest choices and horrible behavior … It's interesting to see how affiliate bloggers are gonna approach the situation," was one of the comments on the Brooklyn Blonde website. Under pressure, BB later clarified in her Instagram Story that she was "not aware" of what happened and was under contractual obligation with Everlane to promote their products.

In the days of rampant pandemic, this particular kind of practiced cluelessness has drawn ire, as the Page Six-labeled #covidiot Arielle Charnas experienced firsthand. Almost overnight, consumers went through the cultural climate change and emerged on the other side, more receptive to brands' and influencers' positive actions and more ready to scrutinize the perceived negative ones. Selfishness, insensitivity, inequality, lack of empathy and compassion, and failure to read the room are quickly socially shamed.

This is the new backdrop for brand strategy. Radical individualism is out, social connection is in. Brand focus is not on the end customer, but on the communities they belong to. Just as personas made individual consumers visible, the new brand methodology makes visible consumer communities and their co-dependencies and influences. New focus of engagement plans is not just on the brand actions, but on their secondary effects. Pre-pandemic consumer-centric brand strategy is now society-centric strategy.

Against this new backdrop, there are the 4Cs of the modern brand: content, community, curation, and collaborations. They impact how a company defines and executes their brand strategy; launches and markets its products and services; and captures, distributes, and delivers value to its customers.

Community

A retailer needs to encourage social connections among its customers. These social connections will become its primary source of value and the key driver of competitive advantage. Social connections work best when created around an audience's preexisting passion, hobby, or interest. High-design bicycle wear brand Rapha positions itself as a "vibrant ecosystem for road riders around the world." Its belief that cycling transforms lives translates into the series of local Rapha Cycling Clubs, where cycling enthusiasts can gather for events, rides, and races, and to bond with others.

During the global pandemic, a brand community quickly went from a "nice to have" to a "must have." It doesn't matter what category a brand is in – it has to find a way to put forward its social mission and values, which are the gel for a community. For brands that already maintain communities, the next step is to activate it more, and more often. Marc Jacobs' WFH and Drawn Together, and GANNI Talks are examples of capitalizing on a brand's own creative community. Or, MeUndies is these days featuring customers willing to share selfies wearing MeUndies products on Instagram. David Zwirner gallery partnered with the wider gallerists' community and launched Platform: New York, an online initiative to feature artists from 12 NY-based galleries. Allure magazine activated its community of stylists, makeup artists, photographers, and hairstylists. Or, going beyond its immediate readership, *TIME* magazine launched TIME for Giving, a community of those keen to provide assistance to a list of charities and causes in need. The key here is for brands to stop thinking about their community just as top-of-the-funnel tactic, and instead consider it as a long-term, bottom-of-the-funnel strategy (bonding, advocacy, loyalty). Next step is to define and focus on the most valuable customer communities. Community management overall has to be more personal. For example, high standard of customer service in physical retail stores can translate in the equally high-standard customer service via WhatsApp, Zoom, and chat.

Content

Content created by a retailer generates value even before a single product purchase or use of service. California-based fashion apparel brand Dôen creates social networks around its proprietary content. The brand prides itself in selling "thoughtfully designed clothing by women, for women." This is Dôen's value proposition, and it consistently delivers it through its product design, events, and its blog journal, where Dôen profiles the extraordinary stories of community members that others can have conversations around.

Across categories, brands have been pivoting to livestream and lifestyle content en masse. Spurred by Instagram Live, every brand these days is in the business of enriching our lives – through recipes, daily meditations, virtual exercises, design hacks to fix our living quarters, life coaching, movie lists, poetry reading, puppy photos, and hobbies. While it may feel overwhelming at times, this lifestyle content pivot is a good thing: it moves the brands away from product marketing and forces them to explore, define, and capitalize on their cultural and social role. During the February lockdown in China, hashtags #StayInFashionGuide and #StayInPajamaContest drew audience of hundreds of thousands. Stay-in style manuals on WeChat, put forward by KOLs, promoted at-home stylish living and solicited "share your look" submissions on Weibo and held #WorkFromHome outfit contests. While situational, these calls to action open up agile content opportunities post-crisis. There's also a welcome content shift toward live programming and away from polished campaign imagery. Brands are currently asking artist and photographer friends to help them shoot new content from their homes, or asking their community to create something new every week, like Alexander McQueen did with McQueen Creators. Brands will hopefully embrace this lo-fi approach, and put forward scrappy, live, and real content focused on communal watching and socializing. Community-oriented content tends to do better at the moment (versus the polished influencer one), as the currently predominant memes and aesthetic language demonstrate.

Curation

With their marketing budgets on freeze and their campaign content in a distant future, Spring 2020 became a perfect time for brands to embrace the role of curators and bring forth their unique POV on everything, from food to film and theater, to architecture and pop culture. There has never been a better moment for a trip down the memory lane and for opening up the product archives. Very few brands are doing this (instead, they opt for tiresome PSAs). In contrast, Rihanna, ever my favorite, launched Fenty Social Club on Insta Live with performances and DJ sets. Somewhat far-fetched is the attempt of an Amsterdam hotel to bring the Easter weekend experience into your home, complete with a curated welcome basket mailed in and virtual concierge on call. With a little better to do, indulging in this hospitality-at-distance expert curation is not completely unreasonable. Airbnb is already doing it with its newly launched online experiences. On a more tangible level, fashion retailers can quickly reskin their landing pages to put forward tops suitable for those frequent Zoom calls. Curation plays a key role here: within a retailers' entire inventory, ask what are the especially Zoom-able items that consumers will gravitate toward? What are the comfortable bottoms to go with them? What is considered a desirable outfit in these days of working from home is new, and retailers can curate the best combos. Discounts have to follow the same curatorial logic that makes sales seem exclusive and special (e.g. "archive sale"), rather than inventory offloading.

Collaborations

A good rule of thumb for brands is to ask what else your customers are wearing, reading, listening to, experiencing, and talking about in addition to your products or services. A retailer's relevance is greater if it is culturally amplified. IKEA's collaboration with streetwear brand Off-White aims at designing an affordable furniture collection for millennials to help them create their first home. More importantly, it reflects the broader taste and aesthetics of their joint audience.

At some point in April 2020, I saw that Supreme collaborated with Lamborghini. While we may be well past the time when a fashion collab can excite anyone, the new breed of collaborations are springing up. They go beyond short-term commercial and PR buzz toward something with a greater social impact and no less buzz. Dairy company Chobani partnered with coffee seller Trade to support the community of independent coffee roasters. The effort is spurred by the common belief of Chobani and Trade that food (and coffee) can be a force for good. In a similar collaborative vein, aperitif company Haus launched The Restaurant Project, where it partnered with a selected group of restaurants across America to co-create nine aperitifs with their chefs. Hundred percent of profits go to the restaurants. Collaborations like these will become new Supreme + X.

Brands eventually recognized that the coronavirus crisis is not a short-term acute emergency. It was a call to action for companies to pivot and hit a hard reset on the way they do business. The jobs to be done for a brand, going forward, are communal and social, and the business success is defined through how much a company supports other companies, how much it improves lives of their customers, how much good it does to its community, and what kind of society it reflects.

Beyond these four pillars of the modern brand strategy, there is also a layer of novel implementation approaches. Courtesy of direct-to-consumer brands, industries across the board are rapidly changing how they run their business and set up their supply chain, operations, distribution, and marketing. Nike is the most recent example: their direct-to-consumer business is currently at 30 percent. The company is looking to increase it, hiring a data-savvy new CEO and pulling their products from Amazon. Traditional companies are subsuming direct-to-consumer practices, and luckily, they have a playbook to work off.

Less, but better

A number of DTC brands launched with only a handful of product SKUs, and turned it into a competitive advantage. Mattress brand Casper currently offers three types of mattresses, which is in stark contrast with traditional mattress brands that confuse their customers with limitless choice and no clear benefits of any. Despite its low IPO valuation, Casper achieved brand prominence by "owning sleep" and offering adjacent product categories, like CBD, lamps, bed frames, and bedding.

Obsession with data and customer segmentation

Direct-to-consumer model can only work if companies know who their customers are. Granular customer segmentation allows precision targeting, leads to better retention, and higher-value customer acquisition. Best approach here is to go beyond demographic and psychographic, and build taste profiles, like Netflix and TikTok do. Then, we will know which products appeal to the biggest number of customers, what product combinations drive the greatest retention, and which product entry points work best in terms of cross-sell and customer lifetime value.

Strategic use of physical retail

In the past seven years, physical presence of online-first brands rose 1,000 percent in the top 300 malls in America. As of October, there were 19 traditional retail bankruptcies in 2019. The challenge is not that physical retail is "dying," but that the brands that are using it non-strategically are. Strategic use means moving away from thinking about it as a sales and distribution channel, and defining its role in relation to a company's business and brand goals, and in terms of "jobs to be done" with regard to its audience and its community.

A clear aesthetic POV

A combination of Instagram aesthetic and the fact that a lot of DTCs work with the same branding agencies gave rise to a very distinct DTC aesthetic. Although we are well past the saturation point of millennial pink and avocado green, DTC brands that stand out are those like Tracksmith and Aesop, which rooted their brand aesthetic into their brand purpose.

Innovative marketing. There's PR, and then there is smart marketing. The former works around Instagrammable destinations, and the latter around understanding how to recognize and nurture a community. Patagonia successfully did this even before "DTC" was a term; today, it's Rihanna that leads the way.

Even as DTC brands enter a new stage of scrutiny, direct-to-consumer practices are here to stay. In the modern brand landscape, they are quickly becoming the best competitive advantage a company can have. Another competitive advantage is for brands to become as much pro-social as they are pro-economic.

In the future, all brands will be B corps

Crises are great truth-tellers. Brands are, in real-time, going through the crash course in social responsibility, and there are already winners and losers. Winners acknowledge what their consumers are going through. Losers are pitching Mother's Day sales and charging premium for medical masks on eBay.

Crises tell the truth about a company. They expose organizational and operational strengths and weaknesses. They challenge leadership. They bring on business disruption, revenue drops, layoffs, and the pressure to reduce expenses and find new ways of making money.

Crises also offer a creative toolbox. They force thinking and acting differently, and force businesses to address problems in new ways. In the process, a business may stumble upon a great new idea, discover an unexpected revenue stream, take a risk it was too cautious to consider before, or find a way to be closer to the community it serves.

Here is what works

Put strategy behind your brand

The first step in any good brand communication is always to acknowledge your customers' needs. All of us right now need some inspiration and uplifting communication. "Get up and get dressed for a positive state of mind" by fashion brand Simon Miller works better than "shop 50% off." In the bizarre display of tone-deafness, Armani Beauty is offering 20 percent off, with a code BLOOM. How about code COVID? In contrast, DTC brands that lead the way. On the Bright Side is a new digital series revolving around food, art, and wellness, launched by olive oil producer Brightland: "In these times of uncertainty, we hope we can still inspire you to continue #livinginagoldenstate." There's also Joycast, which is a free text line from a swimwear brand Summersalt, sharing meditation videos, GIFs, self-care ideas, and general hope. Brightland and Summersalt succeed because their output isn't about them. They also succeed because they use the tone of voice that's uniquely their own.

Distribute your expertise in a new way

Brands' survival depends on their ability to package and deliver their expertise beyond their original business model. Even if consumers are not spending at the moment, they still seek acknowledgment, inspiration, advice, guidance, education, and entertainment from brands. What once was a value-add is now a brand's lifeline. This doesn't mean that every brand should put up meditation videos and playlists of monks chanting. It means that it needs to lean into its own expertise – be it finance and economics, manufacturing, supply chain management, operations, or Instagram creative. Offer business development courses centered on remote working; help startup founders to become financially literate. Every company has a number of areas of expertise. Capitalize on them. We're seeing this with fitness companies sharing their expertise through online classes and also fitness regimens, cookware companies leading brand actions with recipes, food companies putting forward a healthy outlook, and hospitality companies delivering perks like sound baths at a distance. There's a massive opportunity for other verticals to capitalize on the shift from products to content, from events to subscriptions, from transaction to inspiration, from buying to socializing. Consider it a necessary business adjustment.

Amp up your services

A number of restaurants, pharmacies, grocery shops transformed into drive-throughs. Revenue from food delivery overtook dining on premises even before the coronavirus pandemic, a trend that is only accelerating. It is also getting more nuanced. Online shopping sites will take a cue from theme parks, ski resorts, fitness studios, and some restaurants who provide variable ticket pricing per date, time, or location, and offer discounts for less busy days and charge extra for peak times. They will move beyond rigid ordering and delivery process and create a more flexible and a more tiered program that ranges from high-end concierge care to basic delivery, and that is also customized per what's in one's cart. There's also need to go beyond just-in-time systems, which are convenient and cost effective, but fragile. AI will play a role in projecting demand in crisis – something that supermarkets didn't have on their disposal this time around. A more flexible thinking applies to online orders and deliveries across industries, from fashion apparel to home decor to pet care to wellness and beauty. The entire area of supply and demand and customer service will rapidly innovate, driven by current inefficiencies and bottlenecks.

Create a new market

When a New York City lockdown started, I begged both my facialist and my hair coloring guy to start the "how to" instructional video series. It sadly didn't happen: my facialist has two young kids to homeschool and my hair colorist is French. But the market for remote beauty care is immense. Chances are that it will stay that way once the pandemic is over, with far-flung audience wanting easily accessible skincare and haircare expertise. Tmall and Shanghai Fashion week partnered on an entirely livestreamed, "see now, buy now" fashion week, where designers and brands present their upcoming collections directly to 800 million active users. That's a game changer. Or, Metropolitan Opera started nightly live-streaming its past performances, which is both a public service and a potential way to expand its market and build new revenue stream. Chef Massimo Bottura, from GUCCI's new LA restaurant, is streaming cooking lessons, "Kitchen Quarantine," from his own kitchen. Beyond the pandemic, this kind of content and chef exposure can be a great restaurant marketing tactic and a value-add. In an accelerated future scenario, opt-in livestreaming may become a preferential mode of advertising for lifestyle brands: tune in and see live entertainment and demonstration of a cookware, an outfit, or a way to apply beauty products.

Put social responsibility, sustainability, and corporate transparency at the forefront

Personal experience of hardship makes a difference, and there is hardly a better time to accelerate brands' corporate transformation toward greater sustainability, more transparent corporate governance, and more socially responsible operations. Just as those living in poor countries feel the effects of climate crisis more disastrously than those living in the developed ones, we are becoming more attuned to global emergencies and to the role of our social, politics, and economic institutions in addressing them. We expect our brands to embrace their social responsibility and act on it. Every brand should start thinking like a B Corp.

Activate behavioral contagion. Coronavirus pandemic will hopefully give rise to another form of contagion: social and behavioral. Smoking rose and fell, thanks to it; and some activities and areas, like food and sustainability, are subject to it. We are all fasting, juicing, and doing lymphatic drainage massages. If our neighbors install solar panels, we do it, too, according to Robert Frank, a professor of management and economics at Cornell University. Our instinct to imitate and conform should be used for good (the hope is that buying Zara may one day become as uncool as smoking). Right now, we are seeing examples of social shaming for exhibited lack of social distancing; once the pandemic is over, brands can do social good by encouraging behavioral mimicry (and not just in terms of Instagram aesthetic). Brands with already existing communities, like Glossier, Doen, or Tracksmith, can use peer pressure to impose positive social action. But any brand with a customer base, from Coca-Cola to Unilever to LEGO, can also mobilize peer pressure. Peer pressure changes both our behavior and the way we view the world and is a powerful tool toward more generous, responsible, and compassionate behavior.

Recognize that, for your customers, a slower pace of life is a good thing

Before the global pandemic, it was popular to discuss the damage of social media to our brains, psyches, and social lives. Artist Jenny Odell wrote a book titled *How to Do Nothing*, about resisting the attention economy. Doing nothing is what most of us don't know how to do. This pandemic is a good opportunity to learn it. We all loved hearing about the benefits of wasting time and the dangers of hustle porn. Now it's the time to embrace it. Our belief that we are too busy to cook, exercise, sleep, watch TV, see a doctor, shop for clothes, or get over a jet lag led to an entire economy based on out-sourcing and delivering these services. We will become busy again, and we should use this forced time off to create a more balanced existence. In it, we can, free of guilt, set the time aside for cooking, going for a walk, checking in on friends, and helping the elderly people. Brands can enforce this narrative shift through their advertising creative: don't show busy professionals, show someone cooking with their grandmother who survived coronavirus epidemic, thanks to the protection of her community.

Capitalize on restraint as the new aspiration

Macroeconomic changes following the coronavirus crisis will undoubtedly enforce economic restraint. Our current social distancing may enforce a societal one. We may become more likely to consider the impact of our individual actions on our community and be aware of collective benefits (or lack thereof) of our decisions. Brands can capitalize on restraint as the new aspiration by putting forward social values of generosity, compassion, and gratitude, and acting on them through their content, communication, and brand behaviors. There are car companies encouraging drivers to stay off the road, and travel companies encouraging people not to travel. This is a social service that should continue post-crisis.

Shift from the outside to the inside

If the latest trend in the modern travel is any indication, the affluent travel for learning, not leisure, and for transformation, and not thrill. Fixing broken pottery, enjoying rituals, or retreating to a monastery required a trek across the world. But they can also be practiced at one's own home. It's good for our planet if we stay in. It's good for us to sit quietly. We should learn both. We may recognize the superficiality, mimicry, impermanence, and stupidity of chasing the latest Instagrammable street, neighborhood, or vista. In contrast, livestreamed sound baths or at-home recreation of Japanese listening bars may bring us equal delight and save the planet and our money. Brands can play a big role reducing the thrill of chasing ever-new experiences, and helping us absorb better the experiences we already had. These experiences can be both communal and personal (a reliving of the, for example, London Olympics, a SuperBowl, that Berlin trip, or the vacation from last summer). Partner with content producers and curate branded compilations of movies and other content for your customers to watch at home.

Consider launching a new product line

In 2017, the global market for "incident and emergency management" was valued at $75.5BN. By 2025, it's projected to reach $423BN. Brands from Pottery Barn to Naked to startups are launching their survival kits. It may become something in every brand's product portfolio going forward.

Note

1 Thanks to Jessica Davidoff, Founder and CEO of management consulting company Spezzatura, who came up with the idea of GMO to describe growth of some of the DTC brands.

Bibliography

https://www.youtube.com/watch?v=l3jjKuTAPHA
https://www.profgalloway.com/yogababble
https://theconversation.com/with-federal-funding-for-science-on-the-decline-whats-the-role-of-a-profit-motive-in-research-93322

https://pitchbook.com/news/articles/how-venture-capital-is-hurting-the-economy

https://www.nytimes.com/2019/10/27/nyregion/nyc-amazon-delivery.html

https://www.theverge.com/2019/12/2/20986298/cyber-monday-black-friday-amazon-effect-recycling-cardboard-shopping

https://www.nytimes.com/2019/09/05/us/amazon-delivery-drivers-accidents.html

https://kenney.faculty.ucdavis.edu/wp-content/uploads/sites/332/2018/11/Unicorns-Chesire-cats-and-new-dilemmas-of-entrepreneurial-finance-1.pdf

https://cdn.musebycl.io/2020-02/Mamba Forever | Nike.mp4

www.vintageadbrowser.com/coke-ads-1970s

https://twitter.com/MusaTariq/status/1229624988820357121?s=20

https://en.wikipedia.org/wiki/Think_different

https://en.wikipedia.org/wiki/1984_(advertisement)

https://stockx.com/supreme-clay-brick-red

https://www.grailed.com/listings/808069-supreme-supreme-x-everlast-punching-bag

https://www.profgalloway.com/yogababble

https://www.coca-colacompany.com/au/faqs/what-happened-to-coke-life-

https://www.cnn.com/travel/article/qantas-new-york-sydney-flight-record-scli-intl/index.html

https://www.youtube.com/watch?v=1hlzKN8Hlng

https://www.thecut.com/2020/03/will-the-millennial-aesthetic-ever-end.html

https://lebijou.com/covid19

https://www.independent.co.uk/life-style/gadgets-and-tech/silicon-valley-billionaires-buy-underground-bunkers-apocalypse-california-a7545126.html

https://www.ft.com/content/afe67b5c-fea0-11e6-8d8e-a5e3738f9ae4

https://www.ft.com/content/9d0d917e-68aa-11ea-800d-da70cff6e4d3

https://www.nytimes.com/2020/03/26/opinion/coronavirus-meaning.html

https://www.thecut.com/2020/03/cory-booker-is-the-visionary-instagram-poet-we-need.html?utm_medium=s1&utm_source=tw&utm_campaign=thecut

https://qz.com/1812670/a-design-trends-forecaster-calls-the-coronavirus-an-amazing-grace-for-the-planet/

https://twitter.com/taylorlorenz/status/1244483577707999232?s=12

https://twitter.com/arielkaminer/status/1243540197834448897

https://twitter.com/andjelicaaa/status/1243906732331618304?s=20

https://www.highsnobiety.com/p/lego-50-million-donation-coronavirus/

https://www.campaignlive.com/article/santa-margherita-donates-1-every-view-its-new-campaign/1678741

https://www.hollywoodreporter.com/news/coronavirus-four-seasons-hotel-ny-offers-free-rooms-medical-workers-1287006

https://twitter.com/tresemme/status/1235655720642719746?s=21

https://qz.com/1826057/us-fashion-brands-making-masks-expose-a-failure-of-the-health-system/

https://www.theatlantic.com/international/archive/2020/03/coronavirus-panic-buying-britain-us-shopping/608731/

https://www.cbsnews.com/news/rihanna-donates-safety-gear-to-new-york-city-hospitals-coronavirus-2020-03-27/

https://www.theatlantic.com/politics/archive/2020/03/social-distancing-culture/609019/

https://www.amazon.com/Sum-Small-Things-Theory-Aspirational/dp/0691162735

https://t.co/omumBIizJa?amp=1

https://www.instagram.com/mist_beauty/

https://jingdaily.com/how-digital-shanghai-fashion-week-will-affect-showrooms/

https://www.instagram.com/massimobottura/channel/

https://www.washingtonpost.com/outlook/2020/02/20/how-peer-pressure-can-help-save-planet/?arc404=true

https://www.amazon.com/How-Do-Nothing-Resisting-Attention/dp/1612197493

https://techcrunch.com/2020/03/26/airbnb-to-provide-free-or-subsidized-housing-for-100000-covid-19-healthcare-workers/

https://www.youtube.com/watch?v=9qrCHIi16vk

https://www.alliedmarketresearch.com/incident-and-emergency-management-market

https://www.potterybarn.com/products/the-prepster-luxe-3-day-emergency-bag/

https://naked-retail-group.myshopify.com/pages/care-packages

https://www.instagram.com/p/B-CkCX5j7WX/

https://www.instagram.com/p/B92tDd_lnSO/

https://brightland.co/

https://www.businessinsider.com/how-billion-dollar-startup-fab-died-2015-2

https://www.cnbc.com/2019/08/18/there-are-now-175-online-mattress-companiesand-you-cant-tell-them-apart.html

https://www.protocol.com/softbank-brandless-shuts-down

https://www.buzzfeednews.com/article/briannasacks/outdoor-voices-founder-tyler-haney-resigned

https://www.brooklynblonde.com/

https://www.instagram.com/brooklynblonde1/

https://www.instagram.com/p/B-XM8OkDtr4/

https://www.vogue.com/article/everlane-union-dispute-coronavirus-response

https://www.thecut.com/2020/03/bernie-sanders-calls-out-everlane.html

https://nypost.com/2020/04/02/covidiot-blogger-arielle-charnas-may-have-ruined-her-brand/

https://www.nytimes.com/2020/03/30/arts/virus-celebrities.html

https://www.instagram.com/p/B-z1h4LDu-q/

https://www.instagram.com/p/B-r2AY5jo1k/

https://www.ganni.com/us/ganni-talks-podcast.html

https://www.instagram.com/p/B-0d5DznKok/

https://www.davidzwirner.com/viewing-room/platform-new-york?gclid=Cj0K CQjwm9D0BRCMARIsAIfvfIZOJX1D6e2mra1c0puZ7lS3lzXhgK0AJGQrmrj3 yvP2N6NUmjV03OAaAkHuEALw_wcB

time.com/giving

https://shopdoen.com/blogs/journal

https://www.youtube.com/watch?v=wXyT4t43S_k

https://www.revolt.tv/2020/4/10/21217144/lil-uzi-vert-rihanna-fenty-social-club-instagram-live

https://homesuitehome.co/

https://www.airbnb.com/s/experiences?refinement_paths[]=/experiences/KG/ Tag:6951&irgwc=1&irclid=X3RVQv3EYxyOUakwUx0Mo38TUkixLm39yTo ATs0&ircid=4273&sharedid=theverge.com&af=49497874&iratid=9627&c=. pi73.pk4273_10078&irparam1=

https://www.highsnobiety.com/p/supreme-lamborghini-ss20-drop-rumors/

https://www.drinktrade.com/blog/roasters/coffee-roaster-gofundme-pages

https://drink.haus/pages/the-restaurant-project

https://www.theatlantic.com/business/archive/2017/11/future-retail/546119/

https://www.instagram.com/p/B-iN1bsjWJG/

Conclusion

Coronavirus killed the modern aspiration economy. What comes next?

At the beginning of 2020, the second biggest air travel story was Qantas' first 19-hour direct flight from New York City to Sydney. The first one was about the woman who reportedly reclined her seat too far. Fast forward, and air travel is at standstill. Getting on any plane, full reclined seat in front us and all, feels like a fond memory.

Coronavirus is perhaps a fitting crisis for the modern aspiration economy. With uncanny precision, it targets all its tenets: travel, tourism, dining, experiences, leisure, art and culture, and the luxury industry. In less than a fortnight, it exposed the vulnerabilities of trading in social, cultural, and environmental capital. "Access over ownership" and "experiences over possessions" make great sense if there is access and experiences to be had. Once the NYC galleries, theater, restaurants, and fitness and nightclubs closed, and all the rich fled to the Hamptons, the city's social, cultural, and environmental capital went to zero.

Along with intangibles like access, experiences, and knowledge, the modern aspiration economy also created a cultural class unto its own. Oriented towards wellness and self-perfecting, this class of self-proclaimed "creatives" (regardless of what they actually do) defies the hierarchy that socially bound the previous generations to their economic standing, and lives the lifestyle of the affluent without actually owning the assets to underpin it (home, a savings account). This consumer class also created a signature aesthetic genre, a number of taste regimes, and an entire DTC economy of lifestyle add-ons.

During the pandemic, they realized two things: chances of perfecting oneself are much better when a person is not shut in the 700 square feet living space; and sharing lifestyle add-ons of the rich does not make one rich. Buying a coronavirus test, booking a COVID-19 hospitality stay in a Switzerland, and having N95 mask does.

The rich belong to the old industrial economy and to the traditional luxury. They own objects that signify stability, security, and durability (real estate, hard luxury, antiques, high-end wine, collectible art). The core promise of hard luxury is its permanence ("You never really own Patek Philippe. You merely look after it for the next generation") and its liquid and increasing asset value. For example, consider a spike in investment in "survival" real estate dating back to 2017. According to Steve Huffman, co-founder of Reddit, as many as 50 percent of Silicon Valley billionaires bought a luxury bunker or a getaway island. Peter Thiel allegedly owns a remote part of New Zealand. When a global pandemic hits, having a remote island is handy.

The coronavirus crisis put in sharp focus the old-school economic inequality. It also exposed the brand strategy that obscured it.

A decade or so ago, brands shifted from increasing value of their products through utility, competitive comparison, and creative advertising to endowing products they made with aesthetic, sustainability credentials, a story of artisanship and provenance, and/or a community in order to give their products identity and singularity. (Virgil Abloh made a career out of it.) An entire market emerged around brands aimed to be perceived as different due to the simple inversion of the logic of mass-produced, common industrial products.

Modern brand strategy focuses on the sociology of things, not people: it asks how to create social markers of differentiation and dominance around products they sell. The outcome is that products are valued on their story, design, and aesthetics: the dreaded millennial pink, environmental creds as a go-to PR pitch, "locally made" as the brand promise. This strategic approach shifted dynamics of the capitalist system from making products (that's been outsourced to China) toward enhancing objects with social, cultural, and environmental value.

When a global pandemic jeopardizes production of social, cultural, and environmental value, it jeopardizes the entire economy organized around it. Most affected are countries with economies organized around making and exporting high-end goods and services, such as food, craftsmanship, tourism, art foundations, fashion. An economy that revolves around lifestyle add-ons makes an easy target for global crises.

The present near-collapse of the modern aspiration economy accelerates its own future. Value that creative class puts on perfecting themselves and their own lives shifts only in form. Scroll down Instagram, and even the global pandemic has, in the hands of creatives, become a tool of self-advancement. Unlike Veganuary, fasting, Mari Kondo or meatless Monday, quarantine is neither self-invented nor self-imposed. This didn't prevent it from somehow becoming self-improving. Restraint has become ethically and socially aspirational.

Any aspiration is a narrative: it's the stories we buy into and the products and experiences we buy to be part of these stories. Once upon a time, American culture symbolized individualism, independence, and freedom through iconography of wide plains, open roads, and windswept hair. The narrative that's shaping right now is the one of redemption by restraint. Journalists, public intellectuals, and Cory Booker claim that a better world will come out of our hardship. Famed trend forecaster Li Edelkoort even went as far as to announce that we should be "very grateful for the virus because it might be the reason we survive as a species."

We have to believe in silver linings because the alternative is de-spiriting. No one wants to come across as self-centered, spoiled, and opportunistic (well, almost no one). So we redeem ourselves by swiftly changing how we present ourselves to the world ("stay at home," says every Insta influencer). This shift in presentation is not trivial: it changes how we behave and our new behavior exerts peer pressure in our social networks, creating a ripple effect. Most importantly, our new behavior changes our self-perception: we start to see ourselves as selfless, responsible, and kind.

In this crisis, the creative class, not the billionaires, leads the way. They are ready to socially shame displays of greed, selfishness, and irresponsibility.

The same dynamic applies to brands. Brands feel the same peer pressure to change their behavior. If Lego donates $50M to Education Cannot Wait, others will follow. If a notorious Italian winery Santa Margherita gives a dollar for each view of its video campaign, others will copy. If Four Seasons provides free rooms to NYC coronavirus doctors, others will do the same. (Of course, there's always someone who fails to read the room.) Behavioral change leads to a change in the brand self-perception. Crisis accelerates it.

This is a socially responsible equivalent of millennial pink. Mechanisms of social imitation and self-perception that created a recognizable DTC aesthetic, everyday taste regimes, and differentiation based on product singularity are also able to make obsolete the economic, social, and political system that has proved inadequate to deal with our global crisis.

There are three targets:

Economic. De-growth as an economic aspiration has, until now, been limited to the domain of scenario planning and conference agendas. After the crisis, the wealth of a country may be understood not only in terms of GDP but in robustness of its health system and its infrastructure to address a global pandemic and other catastrophic events. The pressure is already mounting on companies to go beyond pure shareholder value. Efficiency was considered a desirable business goal until it collapsed, exposing lack of robustness as its fatal flaw.

Social. People are not only individuals but also belong to communities and are members of a society. Their behaviors are shaped by those around them and by collective symbols and stories. The new target unit for brands are a community and a society, not an individual. Modern brand strategy aims to address not just "jobs to be done," but jobs to be done in a community and jobs to be done in a society. "Not for you. For Everyone," says Telfar Clemens. "Beauty for All," says Rihanna, who also donated safety gear to NYC hospitals. All brands have to add responsibility, generosity, and social improvement to both their products and their actions.

Political. From who gets to be tested and who gets a protective gear, to social distancing becoming a signal of which political side one is on, coronavirus is a political mother lode. It makes inequality, exclusion, and unfairness blatantly obvious. It makes equally obvious the need to address and solve these issues.

The future of the modern aspiration is decoupled from luxury, even in its contemporary iteration of luxury domesticity and conspicuous production. This is a good thing. An aspiration that revolves around community, generosity, and social improvement makes our economy, society, and politics much harder to disrupt by global crises. Crises will be plenty, but we should all aspire to act in ways that quickly contain them.

Bibliography

https://www.newyorker.com/magazine/2020/02/10/can-we-have-prosperity-without-growth

https://www.copenhagenfashionsummit.com/

https://www.thecut.com/2020/03/will-the-millennial-aesthetic-ever-end.html

https://www.ft.com/content/afe67b5c-fea0-11e6-8d8e-a5e3738f9ae4

https://qz.com/1812670/a-design-trends-forecaster-calls-the-coronavirus-an-amazing-grace-for-the-planet/

https://twitter.com/taylorlorenz/status/1244483577707999232?s=12

https://www.cbsnews.com/news/rihanna-donates-safety-gear-to-new-york-city-hospitals-coronavirus-2020-03-27/

Index